Flood Your Being with Light

Crystal Ascension explains how channeling universal energies into your physical body triggers latent healing powers and inspires spiritual awakening. By following this guide, written by a spiritual healer, you will communicate with your higher self, break through negative emotions, reprogram unwanted thought patterns, and eventually transform your being into a body of light—capable of unlimited creativity, healing power, and unconditional love.

This book is unique because it focuses on crystals as your catalysts for Ascension. Learn to connect your soul to the univers~ ~~~~ link to higher guidance thr~~~~ ~~~~into crystal vibrati~~~~spiritual energies. ~~~~with empathic energ~~~~and music. *Crystal A*~~~~ complete guide to healing yourself, others, and the planet through raised consciousness.

As the new century unfolds, we are experiencing an incredible influx of energy directed toward Earth. Now is the time to make the conscious commitment to connect with the intuitive aspects of our higher selves. The tools are here, being channeled right now into this planet, for us to achieve personal Ascension. Open to the light and embrace these positive new energies through *Crystal Ascension*.

About the Author

Catherine Bowman was born in Toronto, Canada, and was initiated into metaphysics while still a young girl. Her interest in self-awareness was peaked by an intensely personal experience with the Anna Mitchel Hedges Crystal Skull, which began a new phase of metaphysical interest: crystals. This led her to study under Dr. Frank Alper of the Arizona Metaphysical Society, where she became a Certified Spiritual Healer and Counselor.

Already holding a Bachelor's degree in Psychology and Education, the author is currently working on her Master's while teaching English as a Second Language. She has a busy schedule as teacher, mother, wife, student, writer, and crystal workshop leader, and is the author of *Crystal Awareness*.

To Write to the Author

If you wish to contact the author or would like more information about this book, please write to the author in care of Llewellyn Worldwide and we will forward your request. Both the author and publisher appreciate hearing from you and learning of your enjoyment of this book. Llewellyn Worldwide cannot guarantee that every letter written to the author will be answered, but all will be forwarded. Please write to:

Catherine Bowman
℅ Llewellyn Worldwide
P.O. Box 64383, Dept. K075-2
St. Paul, MN 55164-0383, U.S.A.

Please enclose a self-addressed, stamped envelope for reply, or
$1.00 to cover costs. If outside the U.S.A., please enclose an
international postal reply coupon.

CRYSTAL ASCENSION

Spiritual Growth & Planetary Healing

Catherine Bowman

1996
Llewellyn Publications
St. Paul, Minnesota 55164-0383, U.S.A.

FIRST EDITION
First Printing, 1996

Cover photo of crystal by Doug Sokell, Visuals Unlimited
Cover fractal imagery © 1995 PhotoDisc, Inc.
Cover design by Anne Marie Garrison
Interior illustrations by Tom Grewe
Editing and book design by Rebecca Zins

Library of Congress Cataloging-in-Publication Data

Bowman, Catherine, 1953–
    Crystal Ascension: spiritual growth & planetary healing / Catherine Bowman.
        p.   cm.
    Includes bibliographical references and index.
    ISBN 1-56718-075-2 (pbk.)
    1. Quartz crystals—Miscellanea.   2. Occultism.
3. Healing—Miscellanea.   I. Title.
BF1442.Q35B66   1997
133—dc20   96–36246
                                                      CIP

Llewellyn Publications
A Division of Llewellyn Worldwide, Ltd.
P.O. Box 64383, Dept. K075-2
St. Paul, MN 55164-0383, U.S.A.

Other Books by the Author

Crystal Awareness

Entities Among Us (forthcoming)

*Dedicated in light and love
to the eternal vibrations of
my loving husband, Raouf,
and my child of light, Adam.*

✦

*With appreciation to
Marven & Effie Bowman
for their endless support
and Nino Balbaa
for his computer expertise.*

Contents

This is my truth.

✦

Alexandria, Egypt, 1989
and
Toronto, Canada, 1995

Introduction

Groping along the treacherous, pitch-black incline, I placed my trust in an unseen guide. A strange combination of fear and wonderment engulfed me while high-pitched sounds and colors, real or imagined, penetrated eyes and ears.

When the coolness and safety of the torch-lit King's Chamber was finally reached, an overpowering sensation of unearthly energy enveloped me. I held my crystal toward the pointed ceiling; light reflected from the wall lamps through its prisms. I was conscious of an inner knowingness that, in some obscure and distant time, I had been in this exact spot. There was a feeling that if I would lie in the remains of the stone sarcophagus, ancient initiation rites would be reenacted. The four walls radiated hidden messages that my conscious mind was not yet able to fully grasp.

Sunlight engulfed me after a slow descent to the pyramid of Cheop's opening. It was a jarring awakening. In front of me, Cairo and its occupants presented a harsh sense of reality. The spiritual euphoria of a few minutes ago was in danger of vanishing. I had a choice: would I allow my essence to lose this incredible experience, or would I alter my relationship to the world? Was this city's poverty and ruin an actual state, or merely the way I perceived it? Somehow I must transpose what I felt inside the pyramid with the outside world. Balance was needed. Here was another crossroads: a new beginning.

Until recently, most people in Western society were caught up in predominately physical, third-dimensional expressions. Lives revolved around career, family, friends, leisure, and entertainment. With the current New Age movement, people are now busy opening up to their soul level and beyond to higher dimensions. They are realizing there is more to life than what our five senses perceive. This shift from a purely physical to a more spiritually integrated expression is due to the changing energies our planet is experiencing.

The year 1985 ushered in the Age of Aquarius. New Agers heralded this long-awaited Age of Enlightenment. Peace, love, and understanding were prophesied for humanity. The Harmonic

Convergence in 1987 channeled Ascension energies into Earth. With the unfolding of a new century, more and more of these powerful energies
will be available for us to embrace this evolution.
We are now, right this moment, on the threshold
of a new awakening. Synchronicity can be
achieved not only with ourselves but with all of
humankind, Nature, the angelic realms, Master
levels, and collective consciousness.

Ascension is raising the human body's vibrations into higher frequencies. To achieve the ultimate goal of becoming a light body requires a
shift in consciousness. Now is the time to move
every aspect of our lives into light. Our minds
need to be in touch with the totality of ourselves:
our physical, emotional, mental, spiritual, and
soul energies.

Crystal Ascension is my personal interpretation
of how to deal with the changing energies of the
twenty-first century. It is a guide to help you suc-
cessfully channel this incredible energy system
directed toward Earth. The chapters will direct
you through the various stages encountered
when you make the conscious choice to advance
your awareness into new levels of Ascension. It
will gently trigger the sleeping soul to release
energies into conscious expression. Once the soul
is awake, coexistence can be maintained with all
levels of life. It is a transformation that evokes all
the spiritual qualities of the enlightened ones,

with one major difference: *Crystal Ascension* teaches you the necessary skills for functioning as a spiritual person in day-to-day living.

This book's ultimate goal is to teach you to raise the vibrational rate of energy in your physical body. When this occurs, you will have a new awakening to the totality of your physical and spiritual self. Lower frequencies of negative emotions will dissipate. You will be in a continuous state of higher awareness. You can be the totality of what you were meant to be. I am certain that you, the seeker, will be inspired to set foot on a path to a new beginning, an inner union with your soul and all that is.

You, in turn, will both consciously and unconsciously help others with whom you interact. As each of us progresses in our growth, we simultaneously raise the consciousness of the entire human race and of the planet Earth.

▲

The
Basics

SECTION I

I

Embracing Ascension

At one time or another, each of us has wondered about our real purpose in life. Soul-searching questions include: Why do I feel so alone? Why am I not happier? Why do I suffer such emotional pain? Why are things not working out for me?

The answer to these and similar probing is simple: We have lost touch with our souls!

There is a current trend in our society to join us to the soul's vital energies. Books, seminars, crystals, gemstones, flower essences, aromatherapy, homeopathy, and other New Age techniques are available to help us get in touch with our higher self. But we cannot just experience a healing or attend a New Age workshop and expect our lives to be transformed. Afterward, that elated feeling of communication with our inner self may last for a couple of minutes, hours, or if we are lucky, a few days. All too soon, rapture is replaced by the realization that we are once again out of touch with our inner essence. The answers to soul-searching questions and lasting unity with our higher self can only be obtained through deep commitment, effort, and the willingness to let go of old, negative thought patterns. Then our lives can truly be transformed.

We have the power to consciously accomplish our own liberation from feelings of aloneness, disparity, fear, unworthiness, and confusion. The opportunity to achieve self-transformation is upon us.

The history of this planet cannot be altered. The past cannot be changed. We are given the necessary knowledge to affect the present and future. We are responsible for creating the way we perceive ourselves and the world. We can tap into the energies of Ascension and break through negative emotions and thought patterns that have crystallized in our bodies. Now is the time to open our intuitive centers to our higher selves. Now is the time to commit to change. The tools are here, channeled right now into this planet, for us to facilitate personal Ascension and connect our souls with all that is.

▲

2

Beyond the
Physical

The word *awareness* means being attentive, perceptive and attuned with the internal self. *Conscious* implies a sensitivity to external events and internal feelings. To be "consciously aware" requires the understanding, recognition, and acknowledgment of our thoughts and their subsequent effects on others as well as events or circumstances. For example, if I generate the thought that I will get sick, I automatically draw these vibrations into my aura. If, on the other hand, I repeat affirmations that I am of a healthy body and mind, illness will not be attracted to me.

Like beguiles like. What we think, we manifest, and so we must be very careful to create only positive thoughts. This is done by expanding our consciousness into awareness.

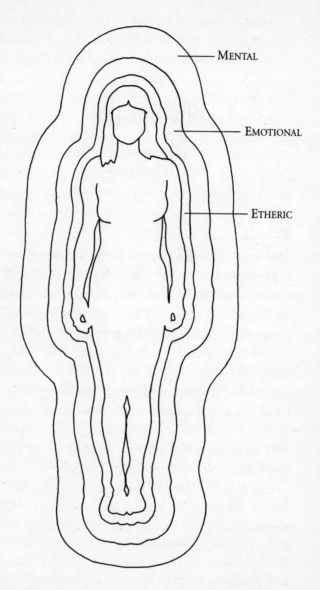

MENTAL

EMOTIONAL

ETHERIC

✦ *The subtle bodies: Etheric, Emotional, and Mental.*

Most people are bound by three-dimensional thinking patterns. Perception does not extend beyond the physical. If it cannot be seen, felt, or heard, it does not exist. There are, however, a growing number of us who believe that believing *is* seeing. We can perceive that other dimensions and vibrations do exist. Many are able to sense the fields of energy that exist around our physical body, aptly called the subtle bodies. These obscure energies have a direct correspondence to our emotions and physical well-being. The diagram on page 6 shows their relationship to the physical body. It is the subtle bodies that need to be consciously explored, then healed and aligned with positive thoughts, to start you on the path of a new beginning. To assist you in this process, an understanding of how these bodies work needs to be explained.

The Subtle Bodies

✦ The Etheric Body

Our skin is encased by approximately four inches of energy. This cocoon or force field, called the etheric body, consists of tiny fibers not unlike those found in a spider's web. Its casing draws in, holds, and subsequently releases energies of the emotional and mental bodies into the physical body. It can act as a sponge, squeezing out positive, loving thoughts or negative, diseased thoughts.

✦ The Emotional Body

The emotional body, lying six inches around the etheric body, stores fear, courage, love, hate, sorrow, joy, and other feelings. When something in your life frees one or more of these contained emotions, its energy flows into the etheric body, which in turn feeds into the physical body.

An example of how this process works is the prospect of a long-awaited vacation. Excitement, joy, and happiness surface. These intensely positive emotions are relayed from the emotional body into the etheric body, resulting in an instantaneous body response. Relief from that annoying headache, a smile replacing the frown, laughter or some other release of tension will occur. The opposite effect would be devastating news. You have been informed that a close relative has died. The message will be transmitted for the body to respond with tears, stomach knotting, indigestion, tension in the shoulders and back, a headache, and a host of other distressing body reactions.

✦ The Mental Body

The mental body lies approximately six inches outside the emotional body. It contains intellect, discipline, judgment, compassion, understanding, imagination, moral sense of right and wrong, and creativity. As the above the examples show, any stimulation can result in symptoms occurring to the physical body. If you are fired from your job, judgment may set in against yourself and your employer. The results of this stress can be prolonged problems in the stomach, ulcers, or a more severe illness. A positive example of connecting with the mental body is an artist who receives a creative inspiration and whose entire physical being fills with an energizing vitality, making life more beautiful and meaningful.

The Physical Body

The physical body is the heaviest of the embodiments. It can be seen, felt, and experienced. This body is the last to respond to any emotions or thoughts. It may take years before a disease actually filters down from the mental or emotional bodies. That judgment against your boss may be eating away at you for months before the ulcer kicks in.

Due to its denseness, the body is also the last to give up symptoms. Headaches, heart trouble, skin rashes, cancer, and a host of other problems do not disappear overnight. The physical body is like a large container holding and retaining its precious contents. Only through an ache or a pain can an unaware person receive the message that something in their thoughts or emotions is not compatible with their soul. In advancing our awareness, our objective is to recognize, understand, and be consciously aware of any negative influences on our subtle bodies before any conditions settle into the physical body.

The Aura

These subtle bodies make up what is referred to as the aura. The aura is an energy field that radiates the conditions of all the bodies. It can extend from three feet or, in the case of Buddha, up to four city blocks. The more spiritually evolved a person is, the more brilliant and extended the aura becomes.

At all times, thoughts from our consciousness and subconsciousness are held on to and are passed in and out of the aura. The subconscious does not know what the conscious desires unless it is told. Likewise, the conscious self does not know what the subconscious has hidden away. Only when the two are working as partners can a harmonious relationship occur.

For example, consciously you may have the thought of wanting a higher paying job, but the subconscious is still working on the belief that you are unworthy, unsure of new situations, and uncertain of your abilities. This old programming will be given free passage into the aura. When that job interview takes place, you radiate a lack of self-confidence. Your speech, body language, and facial expressions will reflect this negative self-image. But, if you truly believe with all your being that this job opportunity is deserved, then your entire presence will radiate this conviction. The new message is released into consciousness. We must be willing to look within and see how this affects external situations.

In the initial stages of opening ourselves up to the concept of Ascension, we need to be aware of the type of thoughts we are generating. When we do become consciously aware, negative, old ways of thinking will automatically be replaced with positive, higher thoughts and emotions.

▲

3
Three's a Crowd

A wonderful trio of expressions exists within our auric field: the soul, personality, and ego. They cannot be seen, only expressed and experienced. When these three are functioning separately there is an overall feeling of disharmony toward self, others, and life. Part of the process toward reaching Ascension is the commitment to blending their energies to bring these expressions into a single harmonious unit.

Three is a crowd. In order for a union to take place, we must first understand how the soul, personality, and ego affect each of us.

What Is Soul?

The question of what a soul is has perplexed humankind throughout the ages. It has no shape.

It cannot be physically examined. The soul has been a concept, even a myth—an obscure esoteric force. However, in this New Age, the soul is a reality.

The soul occupies space in and around the aura. It is referred to as our higher consciousness or the Goddess/God within. This energy is attached to our being by an etheric cord, giving it the freedom to travel into other dimensions.

When the soul's lifeline, its etheric cord, is severed, physical death occurs. However, the soul never dies. When not occupying a body, it is in spirit form. The soul constantly is in a state of learning and progression.

The soul communicates its needs from within. Through the guided meditations and crystal arrangements in this book, you will be able to have a conscious exchange of thoughts. This intercommunication does not necessarily come in the form of words, but rather in many other subtle ways. The soul's expression may be an idea, feeling, or action.

The first thought or first reaction to an external stimuli is that of the soul's. What comes after—the doubting or censoring—is our conscious personality. The soul is the first to jump at an opportunity. How many times have you caught yourself spontaneously saying "Yes, I can do that," only upon reflection to decide the opposite? Our personality vetoes the soul child who is free, innocent, impulsive, and unpredictable. It is too often restricted from truly expressing its needs by the mind, the parent—our personality/ ego. This leads to the question of who is right: the soul child or the parent personality?

What Is Personality?

Personality is the combination of inward and outward experiences. A child is born with certain personality characteristics. Astrologers state that personality traits are assigned to people born under certain planetary influences. For example, a person born in the third Zodiacal sign is a Gemini, characterized by a dual mind, ambition, changeability, and self-doubt. A Virgo is someone who is aspiring, strong-willed, and demands recognition, and so on for the other ten signs. Those who have had a birth chart drawn up usually find their personality accurately described. Therefore, we are given to understand that our soul has chosen certain traits in order to express itself in this lifetime.

The outward effects that mold our personality can be illustrated by a baby who initially knows no right or wrong and has no restrictions, hate, jealousy, or judgment. Interaction with others causes these traits to develop, and the foundations laid by the soul through planetary influences are now further built upon. Parents, siblings, teachers, peers,

and significant others all help to shape the personality of the child for later life. All these influences
have been carefully selected by the soul for the
person to learn and experience.

If father dislikes a certain food, chances are
Junior will as well. If he is prejudiced toward a
particular group of people, the child will see this
as being an acceptable attitude. If mother is an
open, loving person, the child may see this as the
proper way to express feelings.

The personality is further developed through
reinforced responses to learned likes and dislikes.
We acquire habits, roles, prejudices, needs, wants,
and so on, that start to mask over our true essence.

What Is Ego?

Ego, the sum total of how self is perceived, can be
difficult to recognize. It has many disguises and
slips into personality without warning. It is the
material aspect of self, holding inflated or deflat-
ed ideas about personal identity. Just like the
young child, ego constantly seeks approval. Some
people like to tell others about their accomplish-
ments, rights, and beliefs in order to elevate and
feel good about themselves. They are reaching
out for love and acceptance instead of looking
within. Those with a low self-esteem make
derogatory remarks about their abilities. Run a

check on your own ego by observing how often "I have" or "I want" is said, and then try to remove the "I" from your speech. It is almost impossible.

As we progress along the path toward Ascension, we will discover that ego can get in our way, stopping us from seeing our true inner essence and higher self. The most profound way it blocks is by preventing us from being willing to learn from others and to have an open mind. Ego thinks it knows everything. We must open up to new knowledge in order to grow. The solution is to separate ego from personality so there can be an awareness of the soul's true needs.

A Dynamic Trio

Within our "three's a crowd" scenario lie emotions of both a positive and destructive nature. Our soul, personality, and ego are filled with feelings that need first to be recognized, then liberated as we make our way along the path to Ascension. Emotions are tools to help us learn, but they must not rule our lives. When a negative emotion arises, isolate and examine it. Offer it up to the soul for help in understanding its meaning.

We need to step aside from emotions that pull us down and cause disharmony in our lives. We need to clear ourselves of the personality's and

ego's control over us and let the soul's unconditional love pour through. We need to blend the
trio of soul, personality, and ego into one dynamic
expression.

To begin this process of getting in touch with
our soul's vibrations and releasing negative
thought patterns, Nature has provided us with
the perfect tool: quartz crystals. Before exploring
the transforming vibrations of the mineral kingdom, however, there is one more aspect of
human energy that needs to be understood: the
chakras.

▲

4
Chakras

Chakras play a major role in Ascension. They are the doorways to soul recognition and expression. Fully opened chakras link us to the universal forces of heightened awareness. Chakras are centers of energy that are continually expanding and contracting over specific parts of the body. It is through the chakras that energy is funneled into the physical body. With the chakra opening techniques described in this book, your body centers will be resonating at a higher level. Once complete harmony is achieved, the higher spiritual energies of Ascension will be more easily accessed.

The emotional and mental subtle bodies have major control over chakra size, condition, force, and radiance. By bringing these centers into harmony, we are able to link with the Ascension frequencies of the higher chakra levels.

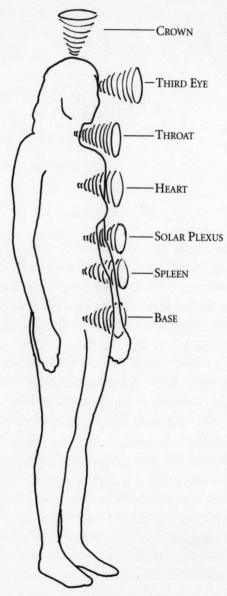

✦ *The first seven body chakras: Base, Spleen, Solar Plexus, Heart, Throat, Third Eye, and Crown.*

For the purposes of this book, twelve chakras will be addressed, although there are many more points through which energy is channeled into the body. The first seven chakras are associated with the physical body. They are the base, spleen, solar plexus, heart, throat, third eye, and crown chakras (see diagram on page 20).

The remaining five centers are the most powerful energies of Ascension. Different sources refer to these new bands of force by varying names. In this book, they are called the higher emotional, higher mental, oversoul, master and creator (I Am) levels of consciousness. All twelve chakras perform a specific function, are related to one another, have individual color properties, and areas associated with physical and/or emotional conditions.

Most people's chakra centers are vibrating as small, dimly colored disks with little force. On the awakened person, they glow in vibrant hues greatly increased in size. When we fully utilize all the body's chakras, both the physical and spiritual aspects of our lives are enriched.

Chakras can be easily stimulated at the etheric level with crystals. Physical and spiritual benefits will begin to occur almost immediately. Creativity increases, decisions are more easily made, self-worth grows, negative preconditioned thoughts are released, intuitive perception develops, and personal needs are revealed. The capacity to speak our truth, to understand relationships, to open up to the vibrations of unconditional love, and to stand up for what we believe in are just a few of the wonderful changes that can transpire. Any pain caused by blocks in the subtle bodies can be reduced and often eliminated. An abundance of energy will be available to heal areas of the body that are affected by stress, constipation, premenstrual syndrome, ulcers, indigestion, and other ailments. In order for us to bring about these changes, an understanding of how each chakra works is needed.

First (Base) Chakra

The first chakra is referred to as the root or base chakra. Its energies are located at the base of the spine. The lower part of the body, consisting of the feet, ankles, calves, knees, and hips, are linked to this center. It is associated with the color red, which has the qualities of strength and power.

One example of an unawakened or imbalanced base chakra is prolonged fatigue. When left untreated, depression can result. The person may procrastinate about doing a task, then withdraw at the last minute due to a lack of motivation.

Another example of a dysfunctional base chakra is the person whose thoughts are completely directed toward material gains. There is no interest in expanding and growing in other areas. An opened base chakra enables us to fully participate in such third-dimensional activities as work, recreational sports, hobbies, and other day-to-day chores. Our soul's physical reason for incarnating in this lifetime will be more understood. A calmness will be experienced; tension and stress are replaced with contentment and satisfaction as goals are met and exceeded.

Second (Spleen) Chakra

The spleen chakra is located between the navel and pubic bone. It has a direct impact on the sexual organs. Orange, the accompanying color, evokes mental responses of courage, self-confidence, and creativity. The second chakra allows self-expression through an artistic endeavor, a professional career, or having the courage to be who we really are. It is also the pleasure center, exciting our passion for life, food, drink, hobbies, and sex.

An unawakened spleen chakra can cause feelings of insecurity, self-doubt, a fear of letting go, frustration, guilt, and problems related to sexual expression. A woman who has difficulty achieving orgasm may have a poorly functioning second chakra. This will cause her tension, feelings of unworthiness, and even a fear of intimacy. In addition, people who have trouble getting in touch with their talents and attributes are affected by this center being blocked. Those who overindulge in eating, drinking, smoking, or sex have an imbalance in this area.

With activation of the spleen chakra, there is clearer thinking, more creative energies, lessened sexual problems, and control over excesses. The soul's energies are able to flow without censorship.

Third (Solar Plexus) Chakra

The solar plexus chakra, located above the navel, has an effect on the stomach and abdomen. Both of these body parts are readily distressed by fear, stress, and emotional excitement. These conditions can lead to ulcers, stomach problems, and poor elimination. This is the spot where we experience the feeling of being punched in the stomach when problems arise that are too difficult for us to handle.

Yellow is the color linked to the third chakra. It brings increased mental stimulation, self-acceptance, and happiness. When fully opened and functioning, self-worth increases, solutions to problems are readily found, and the mind assimilates and discerns at a faster rate. Instead of backing away from things, we are able to put everything into proper perspective. We can more readily draw on our souls' energies to help complete tasks and be more productive. People working with a balanced solar plexus are in control of their emotions and situations and can bring their creative and intellectual forces into focus.

Fourth (Heart) Chakra

The heart chakra, located between the breasts, has a direct relationship to the physical heart. Its green shading suggests healing, balance, and love. It is the link between the personality and the soul.

A person with an opened heart chakra has the capacity to give and receive unconditional love. Such a love is one that does not try to control, manipulate, or change, and does not hold any expectations of receiving something in return. Unconditionally loving people can project healing energies to everyone and everything around them. They are a joy to be with, and they uplift others' spirits by radiating feelings of total acceptance. Even their homes are filled with these vibrations: plants, crystals, cooking, decor—anything that energy has been put into—contains and reflects this pure love. The heart chakra is the pure, trusting love of the soul. It is an inner and outer unselfish love.

A closed fourth chakra causes feelings of jealousy, hate, selfishness, and pain. A person may have shut their heart chakra after a bad relationship in protection against any further anguish. Or, it might never have been open to receive love.

These people are missing out on much of life by their thick wall of self-protection. They have shut off communication with others as well as their soul, creating feelings of incompleteness, despair, loneliness, and lack of balance in all aspects of life. These people are the ones who are most often subjected to various disorders with their physical hearts.

Fifth (Throat) Chakra

The throat chakra is symbolically located over the throat and is related to the thyroid and respiratory system. It corresponds with blue, the color of peace and serenity. This is the center through which we are given the opportunity to totally express our inner selves in complete truth. If inactivated, people cannot speak out about what is on their minds, which is what the soul needs to express. This inability to vocalize inner feelings results in colds, sore throats, thyroid problems, and lung infections. The people may be shy, introverted types who isolate themselves in anger or mask their true essence with rough words or derogatory remarks. These negative expressions serve to cover up hidden fears and insecurities.

On opening, this chakra will bring forth great peace because there is no fear to assertively speak up. For full expression, this person can draw on the energies of the throat for vitality, the spleen for courage, the solar plexus for personal power, and the heart for love; communication will come directly from the soul.

Sixth (Third Eye) Chakra

The third eye is the sixth sense located in the center of the forehead. Its relationship is with the mysterious pineal gland, believed to be connected to psychic perception. The third eye is the center that early humans used to "see" into other dimensions, to sense danger, and link with Nature. Modern humankind lost this power due to disuse. Reactivation can occur, bringing forth the benefits of intuition and spiritual insight. The color indigo, a blending of the blue of the throat chakra and the violet of the crown chakra, enhances our abilities to perceive realities beyond the physical world.

This sleeping chakra prevents us from making clear decisions, blocks creative visualization in meditation, and bars the mind from opening to sensations beyond hearing, tasting, smelling, touching, and seeing.

With activation, the third eye picks up information outside the third dimension. It is the mind's moving picture screen, with the potential to portray images, colors, symbols, diseased organs beneath the skin, past life information,

future events, spiritual guides, and all else that
the eyes fail to register. For most, this opened
center will manifest an increased awareness of
people and events as well as allow more receptivi-
ty to intuitive feelings. This astonishing capacity
of intuition can forewarn, foretell, and guide our
conscious thoughts. Through this sixth sight, our
soul is allowed to give forth its much-needed
communication.

Seventh (Crown) Chakra

The crown chakra, located at the top of our head,
is the final physical link to awareness. It is associated with the pituitary gland, which has control over
the physical sensations and the reasoning power of
the mind. The color violet denotes enlightenment
and spiritual insight. This open chakra gives us the
opportunity to tap into higher levels of consciousness. As its name suggests, it is the crowning of our
inner essence. Without this chakra being activated,
boredom, lack of focus, depression, and a lack of
spiritual growth take place.

Chakras are dependent on one another.
Working in order from the first to the seventh, as
one chakra becomes strengthened, the rest follow
suit. When a person is working on Ascension, all
the physical chakras will be energized to full
capacity. This person is able to function in the

physical world with the base chakra, has self-confidence through the spleen chakra, experiences a sense of overall well-being with the solar plexus chakra, is balanced and in harmony with all aspects of life with the heart chakra, speaks true feelings with the throat chakra, is intuitively directed by the soul through the third eye chakra, and has made a connection to the higher vibrations of Ascension with the crown chakra.

As mentioned earlier, there are five more levels of consciousness that are directly linked to Ascension energies. It is this author's belief that the next five centers are now available for us to enhance our evolution. They will become more and more readily accessed by initiates as the twenty-first century unfolds.

The next levels contain finer and finer degrees of vibrations. The higher emotional, higher mental, oversoul, master and the creator (I am) chakras are the bands of light that surround and filter into our auric field (see the diagram on page 30).

Eighth (Higher Emotional) Chakra

The eighth level of consciousness is our Ascension connection to unconditional love and altruistic

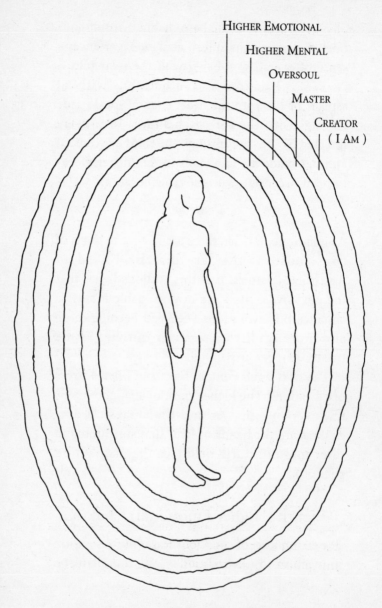

HIGHER EMOTIONAL

HIGHER MENTAL

OVERSOUL

MASTER

CREATOR
(I AM)

✦ *The five higher chakra levels: Higher Emotional, Higher Mental, Oversoul, Master, and Creator (I Am).*

feelings. When we harmonize with this hue of violet green,* thoughts are spontaneously transformed. Any lower emotions like fear, hate, anger, or self-limitation toward ourselves or others are transcended into love, worthiness, joy, empathy, and understanding. These emotions naturally become part of our daily expression and interaction with the world. In turn, our subtle bodies are healed, which causes the seven physical chakras to resonate with more clarity and strength. We are on our way to further acceleration of our consciousness.

Ninth (Higher Mental) Chakra

The ninth connection, the higher mental chakra, is associated with collective consciousness and universal thoughts. Its bluish-green color filters down through the emotional chakra and into the crown chakra. Through this, we receive inspiration, wisdom, and guidance. Solutions to Earth's enigmas can be found at this level. This is where musicians "hear" music inside their heads, scientists "invent," "cures" to diseases are found, and writers "write" words.

Having this wonderful link to universal frequencies of thought and consciousness benefits the technological and spiritual development of this planet. As individuals, we feel more attuned

*Author's note: The hues that I have assigned to Ascension energies are my own interpretation. Readers may visualize them in different colors.

with the creative side of ourselves and are able to lend our ideas and thoughts to enhance the evolution of humankind.

Tenth (Oversoul) Chakra

The tenth chakra is the home of the oversoul. It has a color band of a creamy white shade. The oversoul links the master and creator (I Am) levels to our individual soul and physical body.

It is at the oversoul level that the esoteric Akashic records can be accessed by the soul and the conscious mind. These records hold all the past, present, and future information about our souls. When we are connected to the oversoul band of light, we have a conscious merging with soul. Since the soul knows no limitations and is not bound by three-dimensional time, energy, or matter, communication with others is instantaneous, and astral travel and astral projection are effortless.

Eleventh (Master) Chakra

The eleventh chakra holds the energies of the masters. Pink is the color associated with this high level of consciousness. This is the band where the masters, such as Saint Germain, Hilarian, Solaria, and a host of other heavenly beings, reside. They are available to teach and guide all of us. Universal truths are shared. Healing techniques, soul creation, and secrets of the universe are revealed.

At this level, we are given the opportunity to open ourselves up to higher truths. We also learn to discern and formulate our own solid truths. People who channel the energies of angels, entities, and masters connect to this band of light. It then becomes their responsibility to interpret what they have channeled before sharing it with others.

Twelfth (Creator [I Am]) Chakra

The final level of consciousness is the creator (I Am) band of light. This golden energy is the level of completion. It is the culmination of the energies that are available to us for Ascension. Its band of color arches over the rest of the levels, acting as a protective shield.

When a connection is made to this creator vibration, energies of our physical and spiritual bodies will be completely integrated into one complete being, the I Am. It is a total cleansing and realignment of our thoughts, actions, and deeds. All aspects of self become harmoniously aligned with all that is.

The golden light is the enlightened state of body and spirit that we are striving to eventually reach. All knowledge and understanding is available for us to expand and express ourselves as beings of light. At this level, beauty is seen in all life. There is no darkness or negativity.

With the chakra opening and healing techniques outlined in *Crystal Ascension,* your chakras will be stimulated to resonate at higher levels. Once harmony is obtained by your physical body's chakras, you can start to work on the higher spiritual energies of Ascension.

Reaching into the upper levels of consciousness takes time and commitment. Some of you may already be at higher levels and not necessarily be aware of it. Some may never achieve the twelfth level, but in making the effort to raise their vibrations, they will be more aligned and harmonized with themselves and all of earth's kingdom. Answers to soul-searching questions will be found, relationships will be seen more clearly, the reason for being here will be revealed, and life will be approached with more joy and zest than you ever thought possible. Each day will be a new beginning.

We all chose to be incarnated at this exciting, changing time for a reason. Remember, with every bit of knowledge acquired and spiritual growth undertaken, the consciousness of the entire planet is raised.

▲

The Mechanics
to Ascension

SECTION II

5

Quartz Crystals

Planet Earth is a living organism. All forms of life (vegetable, animal, mineral, and human) vibrate at varying frequencies. It is a natural occurrence for energy to be shared between ourselves and these life forms. Earth is always communing with us, whether it be through crystals, flowers, trees, animals, or birds. It is only human, self-imposed denial and lack of understanding that has shut off this valuable link with Nature. By being open and consciously receptive, we can discover what a miraculous exchange system does in fact exist.

Findhorn, in Scotland, was famous for a group's dedicated, conscious efforts to work with the energies of Nature (*The Magic of Findhorn*, P. Hawken, Harper and Row, 1975). Their results were the growth of oversized, nutritious vegetables under virtually impossible soil and weather conditions. A Garden of Eden was created by these people through working with Nature spirits.

Another documented interchange with Nature was demonstrated when Dr. Lily conversed with the dolphins (*Man and Dolphin*, John C. Lily, Doubleday, 1961). Lily was able to interpret dolphin sounds and translate these vibrations into a language of communication. He rediscovered the lost communication link between humans and higher evolved mammals.

A more commonplace incidence of Nature's interchange is when a pet is uncharacteristically drawn to a total stranger who radiates spiritual vibrations of love. On the other hand, aggression and alienation are felt by these same animals if any type of discord or negativity is sensed from people.

Minerals, especially precious and semiprecious stones, interact with human energies. Some people are unable to wear others' jewelry. They may feel irritable or uncomfortable. This is because these stones have absorbed the previous owner's emotional, mental, and physical energies. Or, if the stones are compatible with the new owner, comfort, feelings of well-being as well as physical and spiritual enhancement can occur. These examples show that an exchange system does occur with Nature. All we need do is to become aware of this communication at a conscious level.

Each part of our subtle bodies vibrates at a specific frequency. However, it is not always at the same level. Some of our energy is affected by old patterns of behavior, disease, stress, deep hurt, and anger. Any of these can cause the emotional body to oscillate slower or faster than the mental body. Or, our base chakra may be more energized than the heart chakra, and so on. What we need to focus on is getting all our energy centers (chakras) to resonate together in perfect harmony. Nature has generously provided us with quartz crystals— the natural choice to help us progress toward Ascension.

Quartz is classified as a mineral. When added to our own vibrations, its vibrations produce an exchange of force fields. Together, whether we are consciously aware or not, both energies merge in perfect harmony to help us raise our vibrations into higher levels of attunement.

Human and Quartz Energies

Comparisons can be alluded between ourselves and natural quartz crystal. Just as the soul expresses its needs through a body, the universal levels of higher consciousness work through quartz to raise the human level of attunement.

Both life forms have a similar energy system. Quartz is a natural conductor of electromagnetic energy. Each moving electron produces an energy field and, when stimulated, moves freely through its crystalline structure. Any interaction with heat or contact with other crystals or various metals excites this energy to be drawn into and through the crystal's body for release out its termination (see diagram below).

Our energies are sensitive to all seen and unseen vibrations. When our hands touch an object, electrical impulses rush from the fingers through the nervous system for the object to be interpreted by our brain. Those who are working to expand their consciousness 'sense' an event before it actually takes place, such as an important phone call, letter, or death of a close friend. Impulses from the higher centers of light are sent to the brain, enabling us to respond to the transmissions.

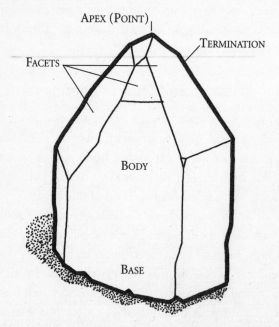

✦ *Diagram of a quartz crystal.*

Like crystals, we are a living energy system. Our vibrations are sensed by the mineral world. The heat from our bodies energizes the quartz and we, in return, receive its charge.

In order to gain a more conscious understanding about our emotional, mental, and physical states, we share our energies with crystals. The joining of our relatively inconsistent vibrations with the balancing ones of quartz can bridge the gap between soul and personal awareness.

Nature created quartz to perfection. A crystal is composed of a latticework of repeated spiraling triangles, duplicating an open left or right spiral within its body. Each triangle is a tetrahedron, an equilateral shape with three sides and a base.

Before the mining process, a quartz point has six facets and the opposite side of its body is always parallel (see diagram on page 40). Facets refer to the flat portion of the body which join together to form a termination. The point is the apex at the end.

Quartz can contain inclusions from other minerals. Iron, copper, chloride, or tourmaline may share the growing space. Colored quartz is produced from traces of these and other minerals. Amethyst is a crystalline variety of quartz composed of silicon dioxide with quantities of iron, making it a purplish color.

Rose or pink quartz contains manganese or titanium. The blackish-gray smoky quartz is

CLUSTER

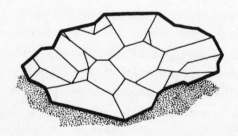

CHUNK

✦ *Quartz cluster and chunk.*

formed from radioactive minerals. Each additional mineral slightly alters the healing qualities of the stone.

Quartz Shapes

There are four main natural shapes of crystals. They are available in clusters, chunks, single points, and double terminated forms (see diagrams on pages 42 and 44).

✦ Clusters

Clusters are a grouping of quartz points that have grown in close proximity to one another and share a common base. There may be two or hundreds of crystals in this formation. Each single quartz has its own unique energy, yet all are in perfect harmony.

Clusters spray their energy in a sporadic yet simpatico manner, with each point continually recharging the others. They can be effectively used to cleanse and recharge a room. Its energies are also used for meditative and specialized healing purposes (see Chapter 8).

✦ Chunks

Chunks are pieces of crystal that are missing facets and points. They are best used for focusing the mind in meditation. They do not make good healing tools around the body.

SINGLE POINT

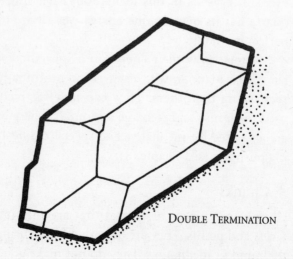

DOUBLE TERMINATION

✦ *Single point and double terminated quartz.*

✦ Single Points

Single points are individual crystals that have broken off clusters. They have six facets with an irregular base.

Their sizes range from less than one inch to several hundred feet. Single points are the most versatile type of quartz because they can be used for healing, meditating, and charging other stones.

✦ Double Terminated Quartz

Double terminated quartz have terminations at both ends. They are powerful tools for healing. They can draw energy in, hold, and release it from both ends.

Quartz may be polished so that the base is smooth, the point is sharp, and each facet is perfectly formed. This machining does not delineate the powerful energies, rather it enhances the crystal for special New Age purposes. These crystals are more expensive than unpolished tools and are unnecessary for performing any of the healing arrangements given in this book. Machine polished and faceted quartz can be obtained in wands, balls, eggs, and pyramids. A brief description and use of these shapes are portrayed below for those people who are guided to work with them (see diagram on page 46).

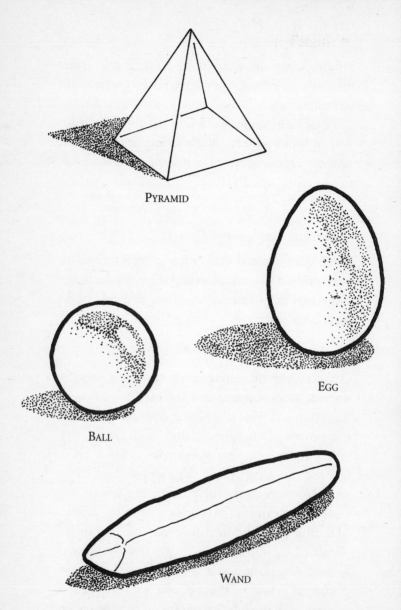

PYRAMID

EGG

BALL

WAND

✦ *Examples of machined quartz: pyramid, egg, wand, and ball.*

✦ Wands

Wands can be used for linking energies of other crystals in healing arrangements. On a more advanced level, their powers are used in radionics and psychic surgery. The sharp point can cut through the etheric body to facilitate a more intensive healing.

✦ Eggs and Balls

Crystals polished into eggs and balls are excellent tools for focusing and directing thoughts while in a meditative state. Many people see symbols or scenes inside these shapes depicting the past, present, and future. Others derive a sense of peace from crystal gazing.

✦ Pyramid

Another manufactured shape is the pyramid. With its flat bottom and four sides, it is aesthetically beautiful and symbolic of the earth's third eye.

If you are drawn to purchase or are given a crystal that has been machined, ask your inner guidance for the best way to utilize its powers. If there is no immediate answer, just enjoy its exquisiteness and patiently wait for the purpose to be revealed to you. Never give up, because there is a divine reason why it is in your possession.

Uses for Crystals

Besides the various shapes, there are many uses for crystals. Personal, generator, and healing quartz are used to facilitate the harmonization of our chakras and to connect our souls to the levels of Ascension.

✦ Personal Crystals

Personal crystals should have an intact point. Over a period of time, their vibrations will become totally integrated with those of your own. This crystal then becomes a very special awareness tool. A personal quartz will resonate with your entire physical, emotional, and mental self. Inner growth will be amplified when you are in a meditative, sleeping, or conscious state.

When selecting this exceptional crystal, it is important to obtain one that has an intact termination. Its size can vary but it should be small enough to hold in one hand. Be guided by your intuition when choosing it. Hold the stone for a few minutes and wait for an energy exchange to occur. Colors may flash on the screen of your mind. A humming sound may be heard. Heat may radiate through your body. Tingles of energy may run up and down your hand. Or, you may just sense a peaceful compatibility. If you just don't feel good about the energy, choose another one. It is imperative that you be synchronized with its vibrations.

✦ Generator Crystals

Another type of crystal is the generator. It should be larger than the quartz used in the layouts. The size is important, as the generator has to be an effective power source to link the crystals used in this book's healing and meditation designs.

✦ Healing Crystals

Healing crystals can be used in healing and meditation configurations as amplifiers of the healer's and meditator's personal body energies. This type of quartz also balances and realigns any inharmonious energies of the person reaching the healing vibrations.

Crystals are a valuable tool in rediscovering the exchange system that exists between ourselves and Nature. In this New Age, they are available to help heal any unharmonious energies within our aura and hasten our connection to our soul. Crystals will trigger the link to Ascension.

▲

6

Preparing to Use Crystals

Quartz crystals are delicate gifts from Nature that require special care and treatment. The following information offers some basic guidelines on what to do after acquiring a crystal. (*Crystal Awareness* has detailed instructions for those readers who want to learn more about this process.) Each person will instinctively develop personalized methods for cleansing and programming after working with crystal's energies.

Cleansing

Crystals, whether personal, healing, or generator, need to be soaked in sea salt and water immediately after being obtained. If the quartz has been received as a gift, use your own inner guidance to discern whether or not the external energies need to be cleared. Some people don't wish to have anyone's vibrations on their crystals.

A soaking solution is made in a nonmetallic container with one cup of crystalline sea salt to one liter of lukewarm water. Any number of crystals can be immersed in this saline mixture. Just before submerging, hold the stone in your hands, open your crown chakra, and request that all vibrations not in harmony with your own be removed.

The length of soaking varies related to the amount of incompatible energy accumulated in the crystal. Sometimes five minutes is enough. If you are uncertain, the recommended time is anywhere from twenty-four to forty-eight hours.

When the cleansing is completed, remove the crystal and rinse under cool, running water. This action will stimulate its electromagnetic energies. Dry with a soft cloth and place it in direct sunlight for a few hours. Your tool to assist soul awakening is now ready for programming.

Programming

Before programming any thoughts into crystal, a clearing of any previous mind thoughts needs to be done. Even if the quartz was obtained from a rock shop or a mine, the process should still be done to remove all thoughts that are not your own. The crystal, like a sponge, will have inadvertently picked up vibrations.

To program a small single point, hold the crystal, point up, in your hand. If it is too large, place it point up on a flat surface and surround or touch the base with the left hand. Double terminated quartz can be held between both hands, prayer style, the points touching the palms. After emptying the mind of thought, concentrate on opening your crown chakra to the golden band of light, the twelfth level. Visualize this vibrational hue of universal knowledge and completion passing through the crystal and filling it with the sum total of all the energies of Ascension.

✦ Programming Personal Crystals

Always base a program for a personal crystal on images of self-growth and harmonization. You may include the healing of your subtle bodies or the balancing and realignment of the body's chakras. Or you can program for the removal of any known and unknown emotional and mental conditions that are blocking the soul from its true expression.

Crystals to be worn on the body as personal talismans may be instilled with images of yourself in perfect peace and harmony. This will repel any external negative energy from entering your auric field. By closing your eyes and concentrating on the energies of the third eye, no unwanted vibrations can invade your subtle bodies. The crystal should be held in your left hand. The following prayer of protection can be recited:

> I am a child of light. I acknowledge my
> entire self being filled with the golden
> light of universal truth and the protec-
> tive energies of the creator (I Am). I
> request only positive vibrations of love,
> peace, understanding, and hope enter
> into this, my instrument to inner aware-
> ness. Neither negativity nor blocks to my
> growth have a place in my life. I am free
> to be the entirety of my soul.

There are an infinite number of programming possibilities. Some self-image programming might be for a successful career, to be a healer, a channeler of information, or for the perfect partner. Always be realistic and completely certain about your desires. Whatever thoughts are projected will come to pass; however, it may not be exactly what is expected, nor will it be immediate. Be assured that if it is in your soul's highest interest, it will manifest. The crystal is only an amplifying tool. Your mind's thoughts are the actual triggers to creating your own reality.

If you ever desire to alter the program in your crystal, simply repeat the above steps of holding the quartz and instilling the new image. To erase and replace an old mind thought with something entirely different, you need to first pass the golden light through it. Then, the stone should be soaked for a few hours to remove any outside vibrations. The final step is to implant the new program.

✦ Programming Healing Crystals

Healing crystals should be programmed for removal of any physical ailments and emotional/mental blockages. Each may be instilled with a mental image of a treated person in perfect health. Later, in Chapter 11, color programming will be explained to further assist the crystal's effectiveness in alleviating unharmonious vibrations.

✦ Programming Generator Crystals

Generators need to be programmed as a linking energy to activate other crystals. While holding this quartz, in the mind's eye visualize a beam of red light passing through its apex and igniting the others like a match. This force is used to connect crystals in healing and in meditation layouts.

Large generators, a foot or more in height, can be placed over a picture of the Earth with the mental thought of sending peace to all races and countries. Placed under the base, personal photographs of loved ones who are suffering will be sent healing vibrations. The thought form when combined with the picture increases the strength of the program.

Individual crystals within a cluster may be given their own program, or one thought can encompass the entire family. To program as a unit, the left hand is placed over the base while the right covers as many points as possible.

Suggested programs are to cleanse negativity from a room, to emit love vibrations, to heighten creativity, to remove physical and spiritual blockages, to attract Ascension vibrations, and so on. Because each point constantly recharges the other, a very powerful thought form can be induced.

The points may be separately programmed by placing the right palm over each apex while the left holds the base. All images should be of a harmonious nature since the energies share a common base. An example would be the thought for self-growth, with each point removing a different negative emotion and replacing it with a positive one. Lack of self-worth can be alleviated through images of yourself performing a task in confidence. Fear is removed by the thought of understanding. Jealousy can be replaced with self-love. Whatever you are willing to work on can be aided by the crystal's powers.

Certain quartz require no programming. These special seed crystals are already instilled with specific information that can be interpreted by us. Programs have already been inserted from the higher realms. One famous example of this type of crystal is the Anna Mitchell Hedges Skull, a perfectly shaped crystal skull that invokes profound energy vibrations and surfaces ancient secrets into conscious awareness.

So, if you have a crystal and you do not know what its use is, ask for higher guidance. In this

New Age, more and more of these special seed crystals are appearing to selected keepers.

Further Suggestions

General cleansing should be performed to ensure crystals are working at their maximum capacity. Rinse them periodically under cool tap water to remove surface dust. The stone can then be rubbed with a soft material to further excite its energy fields.

Healing crystals need to be soaked in a salt solution immediately following a healing. They will have absorbed vibrations from emotional and physical disharmony. These energies can contaminate other crystals and could pass this on to another person. The length of soaking time will vary. If you are uncertain, play it safe and let them stay for twenty-four hours.

Crystals thrive on energy from the sun. Try to give them a minimum of five hours of sunlight a week. The sun's energies help to cleanse and recharge at the same time.

Small crystals can receive a cleansing and charging by being placed on or between the points of a cluster. Crystal jewelry gets a boost from being put on this type of quartz. Usually, a few hours is all the recharging time required.

There are many different ways to cleanse, program, and care for crystals. Each of you has an inner source of knowingness that will intuitively be your guide to caring for these magnificent tools of light.

▲

7

Gemstones

The mineral kingdom has played an important role in human life since the dawning of civilization. In particular, gemstones of precious and semiprecious natures have caught humankind's wonderment and attention with their sparkling beauty, rarity, monetary value, religious significance, and esoteric powers.

Every ancient culture had at least one stone that was prized above all the rest. The Orient valued jade for its virtues of courage, forgiveness, and wisdom, along with its varied powers for healing the mind and body. Jade was used as an agent to help reach peaceful unity with the soul. Lapis lazuli was cherished in Egypt for securing soul immortality and the rejuvenation of body tissues. Adventurine was esteemed in Tibet for increasing creative and intuitive powers. Quartz was widely used in the lost civilization of Atlantis as a source of power for electricity, transportation, telecommunications, teleportation, and healing.

The underlying meaning of mineral usage has been all but lost over recent centuries. Only now, in this New Age, is ancient knowledge of the mysterious powers of gemstones being revealed.

This chapter gives an overview on how gemstones can be used simultaneously with quartz (Chapter 11 gives gemstone healing layouts). Purchasing, cleansing, programming, and healing suggestions are given to assist you in tapping into the energies of these stones.

Comparison to Quartz Energies

Quartz crystals have an intricately arranged internal structure that is in a state of constant motion generating electromagnetic energy. Quartz, with its molecules grouped into tetrahedrons, resonates with human energy. Gemstones do not radiate the same powerful energy fields but can be used for healing and raising our vibrations at more subtle levels. They are a softer, slower, and more gentle way of healing the body. The side effects are less but the process takes longer. They do not project their vibrations to the degree that quartz does. Unlike quartz, color rather than shape is important.

Gemstone color and resonance can be directed toward healing specific parts of the body. While they do not replace the multipurpose effectiveness of clear crystal, stones can be used separately or in conjunction with quartz. Because all crystals have a simpatico structure, the application of gemstones can enhance the powerful properties of quartz.

Purchasing

The most economical way to buy gemstones is in their natural tumbled form from rock and mineral shops. Machining has polished and removed all rough edges, leaving the stones less than one inch in size. This smallness allows them to be comfortably placed over any part of the physical body.

A particular color or shape may attract you, so try to be receptive to any inner feelings when making selections. Most people will experience the same intensity of knowing which stone is calling out to them as when choosing crystals.

Cleansing and Clearing

After obtaining a gemstone, pass a mental thought of the golden light of the creator (I Am) level of consciousness through it. You can do this by either placing the stone directly over the third eye or in the palm of the left hand. Then, cleanse it.

Whether the stone is quartz, tourmaline, jade, or aquamarine, it requires soaking in a sea salt and water solution. Like quartz, the immersion time is dependent on how much negativity you feel is in the stone. After use in healing layouts or meditation exercises, base the soaking time on how much negativity was released (usually 24–48 hours are needed). For newly obtained ones, allow at least twenty-four hours for cleansing to ensure all incompatible vibrations are removed.

The stones can be energized in direct sunlight or by placing on clear quartz clusters. Periodic checking for a stone's strength can be done by simply holding it in your left hand and feeling its energy. If none is emitted, then more recharging is required.

Programming

Since the shape of tumbled stones is not the same as quartz, having no terminations, its programming is not as complicated. The mental thought is not amplified out an apex so the stone does not require any special programming position. Some suggested guidelines are:

1) After clearing and cleansing, hold the stone in the palm of your left hand or place it directly over the third eye. Close your eyes and meditate to find out how this stone can best be used to enhance consciousness or remove a blockage.

2) Open your crown chakra and concentrate on instilling a program. It may be to heal a part of your body, to increase meditation, to open a chakra, or whatever need that stone can provide. Project this thought by holding the stone over the area that requires assistance. For instance, if you desire to heighten your intuitive powers, than place either sodalite or lapis directly on your third eye while thinking the appropriate mental projection. A ruby can be laid over the base chakra, then programmed for an increase of vitality. The actual placement coupled with the mental thought will focus and reinforce your thought.

3) To remove a program, simply pass the golden light through the stone while holding it either over the third eye or in the left hand.

Choosing Gemstones

Some common stones to heal the body, increase awareness, and promote the ultimate union with the soul are given on the following pages. Each crystal healer will have a varying opinion on what each stone is best used for.

One guideline is to associate the crystal's color to a chakra. Reds would be harmonious with the root chakra, oranges with the spleen, yellow for the solar plexus, greens or pink for the heart, blue for the throat, indigo for the third eye, and purple at the crown. Be guided by your intuition as to how each stone can best serve you.

Gemstones can be worn as jewelry in rings, necklaces, pendants, bracelets, amulets, or ear-rings. They can be carried in a pocket, sewn into clothing, or used directly on or around the body as healing instruments. They may also be used as elixirs to work on the mental and emotional conditions of the aura. The manner in which they are put to work is not important; the fact that they are in your aura is.

✦ Red

Red is an energizing force. It stimulates the flow of the kundalini, an esoteric energy originating in the base chakra. Red physically heals conditions relating to the legs, anus, and colon. It provides a grounding force to the third-dimensional world for people who have difficulty balancing their spiritual lives with day-to-day activities. It also increases vitality and self-motivation while removing depression.

A garnet, worn as jewelry or placed on the root chakra, will assist in alleviating negative conditions. If the negative emotion of anger is experienced, a garnet will calmly dissipate it. Ruby has the same effect. It is particularly helpful in removing depression and grief. When placed directly on the heart, its powers will help increase blood circulation.

✦ Orange and Yellow

The healing and spiritual qualities of orange and yellow can be associated with the properties of the spleen and the solar plexus. These colors can balance out an overactive appetite, remove blockages in the sexual organs, and stimulate creativity.

Orange helps alleviate menstrual cramps and the emotions associated with this discomfort. Wearing the hues of yellow and orange will increase and stimulate any latent or blocked artistic endeavors. These colors are also wonderful catalysts for increasing self-worth. They invoke personal power through the solar plexus.

Some stones reflecting these healing properties are carnelian, citrine, tiger's eye, and topaz. Carnelian is noted for its energies to remove sexual fears. Citrine enhances personal power. Tiger's eye is for stimulating clear thinking and topaz balances the emotions.

✦ Green

The green vibration in gemstones relates to rejuvenation, overall healing, and unconditional love. This color is most effective when used directly over the heart chakra to restore feelings of tranquillity and serenity.

Emerald, malachite, and green tourmaline are just a few minerals holding the rejuvenating, strengthening forces of green. The transparent, clear stones add this ray to our aura, while the nontransparent ones absorb the subtle body's negativity. Malachite, being opaque, is very powerful for removing heaviness in the heart. This distress may be lingering feelings of a lack of love for one's self or for others.

Emeralds and green tourmaline bring in the healing properties of green to attract wisdom and prosperity into our lives. They help open us up to giving and receiving love while attuning us to the forces of Nature.

✦ Blue

Any blue stone such as lapis, adventurine, or aquamarine will stimulate the throat chakra. We will be capable of speaking our truth with self-assurance and conviction. The soul will communicate its needs through the spoken word. The blue color also helps relieve irritations in the larynx and thyroid.

Lapis lazuli will help in overcoming shyness. This stone is particularly effective when placed over the third eye in meditation. Its gold flecks invoke the wisdom of the soul and the higher levels of Ascension.

Adventurine and aquamarine are aura cleansers, clearing negativity from the subtle bodies. They assist in releasing suppressed fears by putting us into situations where apprehensions can be worked out.

✦ Indigo and Purple

The colors of sodalite, azurite, and amethyst invoke inner serenity. Psychic abilities, dream interpretations, and meditations are all heightened with these stones. Soul thought and desires become more integrated into consciousness. Your own inner truth will be more apt to surface.

Sodalite and amethyst stimulate the third eye while calming the conscious chatter of the mind during meditation. When continuously worn on the body, they bring forth a deeper understanding of self. These stones also help to resolve conflicts between the soul and conscious expression while enhancing spiritual growth. When placed directly over the third eye, sodalite can lessen tension headaches.

Azurite removes the confusion brought about by petty, irritating problems. It moves its wearer beyond the third dimension into higher thoughts. Like all purplish-colored stones, it helps to stimulate the crown chakra's connection to Ascension energies.

The stones mentioned in this chapter are in no way a complete listing of crystals. Hopefully, you will be prompted to do some deeper research and reading. Any stone, no matter what its classification, will have a positive effect on your emotional and physical well-being. The entire crystal family is just beginning to reveal its infinite secrets.

▲

Ascension
Applications

SECTION III

8

Beyond the Senses

Meditation unlocks the hidden chambers of the mind. Without inner reflection, there would be little spiritual growth or soul awareness. The importance of training the mind to go beyond the limitations of the five senses cannot be overemphasized. It is during this state that we enter into other dimensions. The lower physical vibrations are left behind; the door is open to the higher emotional, higher mental, oversoul, masters, and the creator (I Am) levels of consciousness.

We receive unlimited benefits from shutting off conscious thoughts. Allowing this freeing, uncensored flowing of our inner self brings about a state of calmness, a sense of inner strength, and rejuvenation of the mind and body. It is a private, individual place invoking inner guidance, intuition, past life information and creativity. Through meditation, you can reach the entirety of soul because the limitations of the ego and the personality are overridden.

During this quiet time, there is a lessened awareness of your environment, sounds become muted, and you experience a freedom from the restrictiveness of the body.

It is up to you to train and condition both your mind and body to allow this escape into dimensions that house the soul, spiritual guides, and the Akashic records. The key to permitting yourself to experience this freedom is to allow your imagination its uncensored expression.

Meditation involves activating the third eye and crown chakras. The seventh chakra is the link connecting the soul to universal forces, while the sixth releases intuition.

We all have hunches but may experience them so infrequently that they are passed off as coincidence, imagination, and lucky guesses. Those who are tuning into crystals, soul, Ascension levels, Nature, and spirit guides are exercising the powers of their third eye. When this intuitive center becomes activated, brief moments of enlightenment occur. The mind becomes flooded with insightful impressions, giving the seeker a profoundly deeper level of understanding. The ultimate goal is to achieve this enhanced state for longer and longer periods of time and to be able to tap into this awareness at will.

Crystals are energies to combine with the latent powers of the mind. They will stimulate the dormant pineal gland and amplify our awakening spiritual energies.

Crystals act as catalysts during meditation, connecting the soul to the universe, the self, and higher guidance. By using them as tools to assist you in reaching an altered state of mind, you will become a healthier, happier person.

Meditation Guidelines

For people already in touch with their inner selves, where they meditate does not matter. It can be done anywhere, anytime—even while walking, working, or performing daily chores. But, for those who have never meditated before, some basic guidelines are as follows:

1) The time and place should be given consideration. Meditation should be preferably done at the same time each day. Just as we have a set time for eating, sleeping, waking, and working, we should schedule our inner time. A quiet, dimly lit area should be selected. Soft, tranquil music may be played to block out any distracting noises. A candle can be lit and incense burned. Create your own private sanctuary with an ambiance that is relaxing.

2) Choose to sit either on the floor or in a chair that isn't so comfortable that it induces sleep. Loosen all restrictive clothing and remove any crystal jewelry.

3) A prayer of protection should be recited before drifting into an altered state. This invocation will keep any negative energies from entering into your auric field. Some say the Lord's Prayer, others have their own. If in doubt about what to use, just ask for God's protection.

4) If you cannot shut off the chatter in your mind, do not become discouraged. The act of sitting quietly with the intent of meditating is all that matters. You are conditioning the mind and body that now is the time for inner solitude. Some days even the most experienced meditators cannot quiet their thoughts.

5) Set your mental timer for a specified length of time. Fifteen to twenty minutes is the recommended length for being in an altered state with a crystal. Later, when tolerance has been built up to the energies, this time can be extended up to as long as you desire.

6) Try not to become discouraged if no sensations or visualizations are experienced. Only with practice will the third eye and crown chakras

come into full activation. Never compare your progress to anyone else's. We each advance in different ways. You may never see colors, past life information, or hear voices. Instead, you may sense the vibrations around you, or just feel peaceful and relaxed.

The following crystal meditations are intended as guidelines to trigger your own methods of reaching universal truths. Through meditation, you will begin to discover all the beauty and potential of quiet knowingness that waits to be released.

Meditation 1

The objective of this first exercise is to facilitate the higher self's connection with the energies of the crystal. This harmonious union will help you to tune into the universe and your soul. You may have the origins of the crystal revealed and how it can best be used as an instrument to assist your growth. Visions, symbols, or voices can manifest, or nothing may occur at a conscious level. But be assured that you will be taken away from the restrictiveness of physical life.

This first meditation will also help pull the left and right hemispheres of the brain together. The analytical, left side needs to merge with the abstract, right side. These are both vital parts of your conscious expression and to exercise one without the other creates an imbalance. The left portion houses our mental pursuits such as reasoning, discernment, and all concrete capabilities. The right side controls creativity, abstract thinking, and the ability to go beyond the limitations of the three-dimensional world.

After reading through the steps given below, sit either in a straight-backed chair with both feet flat on the floor or in the lotus position. Place a personal crystal in your hands and rest them on your lap.

✦ Step One

- Close your eyes.
- Take a deep breath through the nose for the count of three.
- Hold it for the same length of time in your lungs.
- Breathe out from the mouth in three breaths, expelling all the air.
- Repeat this process until you have set up a rhythmic breathing pattern. This slows down the mind's awareness of the body by occupying your full attention.

✦ Step Two

- Count backward from nine to one in a slow, even manner.
- Set your biological timer to bring back full awareness in fifteen minutes (it becomes extremely accurate with usage).

✦ Step Three

- Focus your attention on the crystal in your hands. Envision its shape on the screen of your mind. Stare at it, then look beyond its shape to help focus the left and right side of the brain together.
- Now focus once again on the mental image of the crystal. Try to enter the crystal with your body. You do not need to look for an opening, but may enter from any part of its structure.
- Imagine that your physical body has no gravitational restrictions and is floating within the crystal's structure. Your body should be in a complete state of relaxation. It may take several sittings before this fully occurs. If you experience difficulty in removing awareness from your body, there are many meditation tapes available that talk you into relaxing.

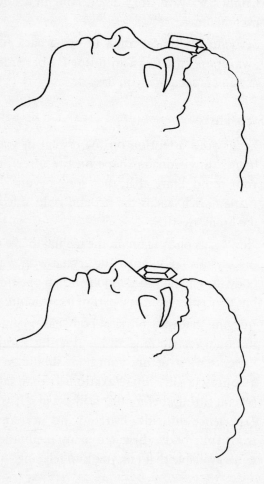

✦ *Placement of crystals parallel to the body.*

- Feel what it is like to be a crystal. Touch its sides. Take note of its temperature and texture. Smell it. Become it. Exert your energies and flow as one.

✦ Step Four

- Stay inside the crystal and allow your mind to wander wherever it pleases. See what thoughts or images manifest.
- When the fifteen minutes have expired, envision your body gently passing out of the crystal. Remove it from the screen of your mind.
- Feel it back in your hands and count slowly up from one to nine, back to consciousness.

This meditation should be repeated until you are comfortable with the process.

Meditation 2

This second exercise will further stimulate the third eye chakra while enabling you to experience the effects of crystal energy directly on your body.

✦ Step One

- Lie on your back on the floor, bed, or sofa.
- Place your crystal, point up, toward the top of your head directly over the third eye. If need be, secure it with an adhesive to your forehead. A double terminated crystal may be

substituted for a single point. Its terminations go parallel to the body (see the diagram on page 78 for clarification).

- Close your eyes.

✦ Step Two

- Relax the mind and body with the same breathing exercises given in step one of Meditation 1.

✦ Step Three

- Focus your attention on the crystal.

- Mentally will your body's energies to flow up from your feet into the crystal.

- Become aware of its gentle pressure, temperature, and weight as you mentally request the third eye to open to its full capacity.

- Envision a closed lotus flower, one that the dawn has not yet reached with her soft, golden rays of warmth. See this sleeping flower in the colors of indigo, a purplish-blue hue. Place the golden light of the creator (I Am) around it. Allow its virgin petals to open slowly in a ritualistic dance, one by one. When the petals are all opened to the light, your chakra will be fully energized.

✦ Step Four

- Imagine the crystal gently being absorbed through this opened center and entering your mind.

- Stay in this altered state while imagining the crystal floating inside your head. Be attentive to any thoughts, images, colors, sounds, or messages that are being transmitted. They are indications that your third eye is opening up.

✦ Step Five

- Close the third eye by picturing the lotus closing up.

- Count back from nine to one.

- Remove the crystal and lie quietly until you are ready to get up.

This meditation may also be used for opening and stimulating the crown chakra. Following step one's instructions given above, you would place a single point crystal at the top of your head with its point directed away from the body. Visualize energy flowing from the stone into the crown and then to the center of your brain. This exercise will act as a connector for the right and left hemispheres and link the soul to Ascension frequencies.

Meditation 3

The third technique uses seven single point crystals to enlarge the chakra openings. They will help balance and align any energies that may be displaced. The crystals must be small enough to rest comfortably over each center when placed on the body. Adhesive tape may be used for securing the crystals to points on your body.

Before beginning this meditation, it is advisable to have completed the first two exercises a few times because you are going to experience new energies. Crystal energies need to be respected. Many side effects can occur if their powers are not properly and wisely used. A headache may develop during or after meditating or healing. Depending on the intensity of the energies, discomfort can last from a few minutes to several hours. The reason a headache happens is due to

✦ *Laying crystals on the chakras, all points directed upward.*

crystal energies flowing into the dormant pineal gland, which becomes irritated with activation. From a metaphysical perspective, your body is saying, "I am not ready to incorporate these new vibrations totally within my energy fields." You may resume crystal therapy after forty-eight hours. Give yourself time for the energies to harmoniously resonate with all of your being.

✦ Step One

- Lie face up on a comfortable surface.
- Place a crystal, point up, over each of the seven chakras (see diagram on page 82).

✦ Step Two

- Place yourself in meditative state.
- Set your mental alarm clock to return to full consciousness in fifteen minutes.

✦ Step Three

- Focus your attention on the crystal lying over the base chakra. Feel its weight and temperature.
- Gently open the base's energy by picturing a lotus flower over this chakra. Color it red.
- When you feel the petals are open, take the crystal into your base chakra by imagining it gently being absorbed by your skin.

✦ Step Four

• Repeat the flower opening with the other six chakras. Use the color orange for the spleen, yellow over the solar plexus, green for the heart, blue on the throat, indigo for the third eye, and violet at the crown. Be sure to visualize each crystal being incorporated into your body.

✦ Step Five

• Mentally imagine a white light being pushed from your base through all the other chakras into the crown. You are consciously directing your energy into the crystals over the chakras so all become linked and aligned. When the energy reaches the top of your head, pass it back down through the third eye to the throat, and so on back to the base.

• Repeat this process two more times.

✦ Step Six

• Relax into the newly-created energies and allow your mind to drift away from the restrictions of your body. Float with any images, symbols, et cetera.

✦ Step Seven

• When the allotted time has lapsed, close each chakra by seeing the lotus flower petals shutting up.

- Count back from nine to one.
- Gently remove the crystals and come back to full awareness, feeling refreshed and more at ease than you have ever felt before.

You will now have a better understanding of how the body resonates with crystal energies. Heat and magnetic flux from the body stimulate the electromagnetic flow within the quartz. Because they are laid in a relatively straight line up the center of the body, the energies flow in a uniform pattern, travelling from crystal to crystal (from the base up though the point of each).

If you felt tingles over any of the chakras, this means that the crystal vibrations and those of your body are intermingling and balancing. This meditation may be repeated anytime you feel that the chakras are out of alignment or need to be stimulated.

Meditation 4
A Pyramid of Light

The final meditation is designed to raise your energies into the higher levels of consciousness. It involves the physical construction of a pyramid of light.

Anything done within a pyramid structure will be amplified. By meditating in it, contact will be more readily made with the energies of your higher emotional, higher mental, oversoul, masters, and creator (I Am) levels. In this light temple, the quartz energies rise up along the sides until they reach the apex. Then, they flow back down the sides, filling the entire structure with crystal power.

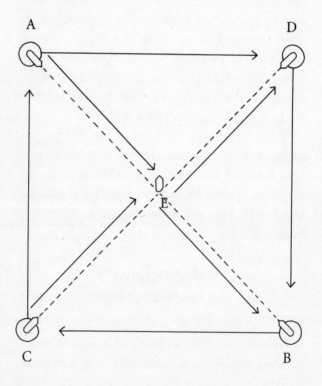

✦ *Layout for the Pyramid of Light meditation.*

Five single points of approximately four inches in length are required to make a pyramid of light. Taking four of these, place each in a bowl of earth by implanting the base in the soil. Leave the points uncovered by at least two inches. These four will be used as the energy source for the corners of the pyramid. The fifth crystal will be suspended from the ceiling to form the apex.

Locate the potted crystals either four, five, or six feet apart in the shape of a square. The size of your room will dictate their placement. Each crystal should then be angled toward the center of the square at approximately fifty-two degrees. This completes the base (for clarification see page 86).

The apex crystal is then hung from a thread in the exact center of the square, point down toward the floor. A small nail or tack can be pushed into the ceiling, or strong tape can be used. The floor-to-crystal measure needs to be the same length as the distance between the potted crystals. For example, if the base crystals are placed four feet apart, then you need to have this apex crystal fall four feet above the floor to complete the flow of pyramid energy. To secure this last crystal, simply wrap the thread around its body a few times.

A generator crystal is used to invoke a connecting force to unite all five. This is done by:

• Beginning at the corner crystal (labeled A), run the generator straight up the imaginary line to the apex crystal (labeled E).

• Without breaking the flow, move the line of force down to crystal B and along the imaginary base to C, then back to E and down to D, and so on, until all the possible energy linkages have been made.

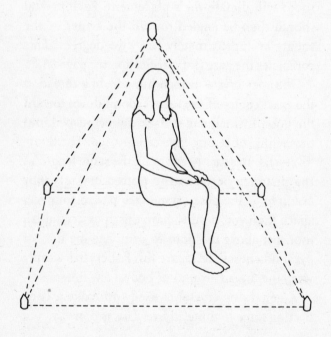

✦ *Physical placement of self in pyramid.*

Depending on the crystal sizes and the structure's dimensions, allow at least two hours for the energy in the pyramid to build up. You may elect to sit on the floor or in a chair within the crystals. Make certain that your crown is centered under the ceiling crystal and that your head is in the upper third of the pyramid (see diagram on page 88).

✦ Step One

- Use the previous meditation routines of breathing, setting the time, and relaxing. No other stone is used for this meditation as it would distort the energy field.

✦ Step Two

- Mentally request and envision the opening of your chakras by using the flower petal method.
- Float freely within the energies. You may actually feel a desire to straighten your spine or rotate your neck. All this indicates is that your chakras are being aligned and centered with the energies of the apex crystal.

✦ Step Three

- At the center of the head, your crown chakra, imagine the point of a violet-green funnel starting to form. Visualize it twirling and gathering momentum as it spirals toward the apex of the pyramid. See it gathering up any lower emotions and whirling them away from your body. Push this vortex out through the crystal at the top of the structure.

Change the imaginary funnel to a bluish-green hue. Have it gather any negative thoughts of judgment, prejudice, control, unforgivingness, and rigidity into its power. See these thoughts being removed from this mental level of consciousness. Push this vortex into the tenth band by altering its color to an off-white shade. See it gather speed and brilliance as it goes higher into the master level. Finally, change it into gold as the funnel completes its journey into the creator (I Am) chakra.

• For further connections to the upper levels of Ascension, reverse the above instructions. Picture the funnel going from the twelfth down to the eighth chakra and then pull the vibrations and colors into your base chakra. This will ground the Ascension vibrations into your physical body.

✦ Step Four

• Allow yourself to go deeper into your altered state of awareness and wait for messages to drift across the third eye's screen.

✦ Step Five

- When the time is up, close each chakra and come back to an alert state.

If at all possible, this crystal formation should be left up. Its power will increase if a generator is passed over its base and up to the apex before each meditation. It is not recommended under any circumstances that the time be extended to more than one-half hour. The brain can become over-energized, causing headaches and disorientation. Use your common sense and intuition by listening to the inner voice that protects you.

After trying these meditations, begin to formulate your own. Eventually you will reach a point in your development when these tools of light will not be needed, but until that time, experiment. The possibilities are way beyond the five senses.

▲

9

How Healing
Works

Emotional and physical disorders are a result of
conflict between the mind and soul. Disease is
the soul's method of contacting its conscious
vehicle. It is saying, "Something is not in order!"

It is not enough just to heal the physical body.
The underlying emotional and mental causes
must also be investigated.

Conventional medicine diagnoses pain and
discomfort as the malfunctioning of a part or
parts of the physical body. Treatment is with
drugs and other therapies. In our current times,
there are alternate methods available that focus
on the personality and the subtle bodies. Some of
these New Age treatments are homeopathy,
reflexology, radionics, flower remedies, crystals,
and gemstones.

This is not to imply that there is no place for traditional medicine; quite simply, however, we need to be more aware of why the symptoms are there instead of just treating the ailment. For example, a smoldering anger in the emotional body that is not recognized at a conscious level leaves the door ajar, inviting a cold or flu into the physical body. Drugs such as antibiotics will alleviate the present symptoms, but chances are the etheric body is already damaged and another ailment is waiting to settle in unless that anger is addressed.

The healing techniques in this book are directed toward comforting the personality as it begins to release old, negative programming. This is done by working on the etheric, emotional, and mental levels of energy. Physical ailments such as backaches, headaches, ulcers, premenstrual syndrome, constipation, rashes, et cetera will begin to lessen. It is not the intention for this information to be a cure-all, rather it suggests ways for the healer to effect and manifest a cure.

All of us are healers. A mother touches her sick child's forehead to check for a fever. Her actions are actually displacing some of the discomfort with love. In all probability, she cannot cure the child with this touch, but just knowing love and caring attention are available can make the little one more comfortable .

When close friends and relatives exchange ideas and share concerns, they heal and are healed simply by being in one another's presence. Dancers, musicians, comedians, actors, singers, writers, and artists all are healers. They provide their audience with an escape from their problems. These special people heal us for a few minutes, hours, or however long we are being entertained. We do not need to be a medical professional, artist, mother, or even an alternative healer to help others. All we need to do is be consciously aware of the fact that we are healers.

The Healer's Role

As conscious healers, we make the universal energies of love and healing available to comfort the soul of a suffering person. These energies will assist the soul to release the discomfort if the conscious personality is willing. To do this effectively, both the healer and the one being treated need to be involved in the healing process. So, if the person chooses at a conscious level to not give up the problem, then we must not judge or blame our healing capabilities. The personality for many reasons still wishes to hold onto that pain.

As healers, we are not medically trained to diagnose diseases. Our role is first to help the person understand why there is an emotional or physical suffering. Next, we make the energies available to that person's soul to release the problem. Lastly, we replace the void with loving, self-accepting energies.

When treating someone in a crystal arrangement, we should never leave that person unattended. If any unusual reactions occur, such as body jerking or rapid eye movement, the treatment needs to stop. The etheric webbing is then smoothed over with the healer's hands.

None of the healing exercises should be done on casual acquaintances until the healer is more adept. Also, they are not recommended for anyone who is on drugs, under the influence of alcohol, or pregnant.

Channeling Energies

We do not heal with our own energies. Instead, we are the channel for the energies.

- Stand erect, shoulders back, head up. Hold your arms, with the palms flat, up to the ceiling.
- Take three slow, deep breaths.
- Open your crown chakra to allow the higher healing frequencies to filter down through your body.
- Mentally ask to be connected to the creator (I Am) band of energy.

- Visualize the opening of your eighth chakra, about one foot above your head, and your ninth chakra, about one more foot above. Mentally project your energies even farther to the tenth, eleventh, and twelfth bands of light.

- Then, imagine the golden light of the creator (I Am) chakra, streaming down through all your centers, into your feet and to about six inches beneath the floor. You are in effect making a rod of pure healing energy.

- Wait for a few seconds or minutes, arms still raised, until you feel warmth, tingles, colors, or however you sense a connection to energies other than your own.

- Put your arms down.

You are now ready to channel healing vibrations.

Healing Aids

Quartz crystals are powerful tools to enhance the energies flowing through the healer. They realign the subtle bodies' energy fields, open the chakras, and promote the conditions needed to stabilize any emotional and physical aspects that are out of balance. The crystals correct the energy that is out of alignment while the hands concentrate and direct their flow. More specifically, crystals set up electromagnetic force fields that repolarize any fields in the body that are out of order.

The universal energies channeled into the healer flow out of the hands. These are used to smooth out and rearrange the etheric webbing with the help of crystals lying on or around the recipient's body. The etheric body, containing energies from the emotional and mental bodies, traps and retains any disharmony. Any uneven flow can be felt with the hands or actually seen by some healers. Temperature changes or holes are the main indications as to where more healing needs to be directed.

Through experience, the healer may find one hand more adept at feeling energy vibrations. Its opposite may be better at smoothing and spreading energy over the body. Or, both hands placed one on top of the other may create the correct effect. The left hand, the one a mother instinctively places over her child's forehead to ease a fever, usually is the soother while the right hand adds the healing power. The beginning healer should experiment with different hand movements to learn which is most effective.

The following explains how the hands are used to discover what areas of the subtle bodies are in need of healing.

- After mentally connecting to the healing energies, stand beside the healing table where your partner is lying down, face up.

- Open the person's third eye chakra by placing your left hand, palm facing down, about four inches above this center.

- Wait until you feel tingles or heat telling you that a connection has been made.

- Next, you "feel" the etheric webbing (about four inches above the physical body) by gently and slowly moving both your hands, palms down, over this surface from the shoulders to the feet. You are searching for holes, heat, or coolness. In other words, you are looking for tears or breaks in the webbing.

- Move up to the emotional body, approximately eight inches above the physical body. Again, you are trying to feel for any breaks or temperature fluctuations. Move your hands, palms down, from the shoulders to the feet of the person you are healing.

- Repeat the above with the mental body energies, approximately ten to twelve inches above the person's body.

- If there were any punctures or temperature fluctuations in either the emotional or mental bodies, the condition has not yet made its way through the etheric webbing into the physical body. Through using your hands, you have the capability to effect a healing. You will smooth out, add, and remove energy.

• Discover which hand is most appropriate for instilling energy and use your other hand to take energy away. For example, if there is a coolness over the left shoulder in the mental body, add your energy through the left or right hand by leaving it there for a few minutes. Or, if there is a hole in the emotional level, spread the energies from the rest of this level over and over this punctured area. For a temperature increase in either body, you need to smooth out and remove energy with your hands by flexing your right hand (or left, whichever you have discovered takes energy away) several times over the spot until an even temperature is felt. When these two bodies (emotional and mental) are in perfect "feeling" order, then you have removed and prevented any potentially damaging energies from entering into the physical body.

• Next, move your hands down to the etheric body. If you feel heat or coolness, you may assume it is either already in the physical body or going to be there shortly. This is where crystals will be of help.

Crystals laid on the body will work on the etheric levels of energy. Their power will also be radiated into the emotional and mental bodies. Use quartz to help correct any energy imperfections that are in the etheric body. You will help prevent them from filtering down into the physical body.

- Where you feel some imperfection in the etheric body, place crystals on the body directly under this area. For example, if there is a hole over the left front thigh, take three similarly-sized single points, and place them flat in the shape of a triangle with their points touching around this area.

- Use your hands or a generator crystal to connect the energies of these three crystals. Leave them on the body for a few minutes and repeat the above action of smoothing and adding energy with your hands.

- Remove the crystals, smooth over the etheric webbing, and work on another area of the body.

- Have the person being healed turn over and lie on the stomach and repeat the above (except for the third eye opening).

- When the healing is finished, gently touch the person's third eye to close its energies down.

Preparations and Responsibilities

For healing yourself and others, certain preparations need to be made. The environment ideally should have subdued lighting to create a relaxed atmosphere. Serene, soft music can be played. Some healers like to have a candle lit to cleanse the room of negativity and promote a peaceful, nonthreatening ambiance. Incense may also be burned. Be guided by your inner voice to create the best working place for you and your partner.

The one to be healed should loosen any restrictive clothing and remove belt buckles, coins, watches, jewelry, and crystals so there is nothing to cause an interference or distortion in the energy fields. This person then lies flat on their back on the floor, bed, or healing table. Ask your partner if any physical problems or any emotional difficulties are present before you begin the examination of the subtle bodies.

Ensure that the one to be healed is comfortable, with eyes closed and drifting into a peaceful state of mind. It is now time to channel the energies through your body.

A treatment can range anywhere from ten to forty minutes, depending on what layouts are used and how much emotional releasing the person needs to let go of. Some people will never experience any overt signs of release; it occurs at more subtle levels for them.

After Treatment

Have the person lie still for a few minutes. She or he may feel cold or hot due to the energies being rearranged and balanced. If chills are felt, cover the person with a blanket. Other possible reactions may be temporary disorientation and dizziness, or calmness and a feeling of being in complete harmony. If the person is emotionally upset, you must help this person to understand that the healing has effected the release of old negative blocks wedged into the emotional and mental thoughts.

Be understanding and encourage this response, as the hardest task is to let go and release our hold on an emotion or judgment on another person or ourself. We tend to hang on, consciously or unconsciously, to unhealthy feelings because they are familiar and part of us. Even though we know this is harmful, destructive, and even painful, it is easier to hold on to a known negative force than to replace it with an unknown. Healing will assist in bringing some of these negative preconditioned concepts out in the open.

For example, a woman still believing herself to be in love with a past partner who left her for another still holds his image, thinks about him, and compares all potential mates to him. She has not been able to forget him and let go of the past. This woman subconsciously feels safer holding on to her feelings of loss and betrayal than to face the unknown future without these emotions. A healing may surface this type of realization for her. Her reaction may be crying as she accepts the need to let go of her obsession with this man.

Another example of how a healing can bring hidden emotions into conscious awareness is the man who cannot forget being fired from his job. He thinks about the injustice day and night.

He projects a bitter image to family, friends, and prospective employers. He cannot let go of his feelings because they have become imbedded into his aura. A healing will help release some of this anger, bitterness, and disillusionment.

As a healer, you need to help people facilitate a removal of negative emotions and then provide a replacement for those feelings when they are removed from their energy fields. When an old, worn-out program is let go, the void has to be filled. To do this, you can hug your partner or lay your hands over the heart center. This fills up the void with unconditional, loving energies. Either of these replacements shows you support and accept the person unconditionally. It is a good idea to have your partner, while still lying down, visualize the aura being filled with the colors of the oversoul's creamy off-white color.

When you wish to cease channeling healing energies, request the closing of your crown chakra. Wash your hands and mentally pass a cleansing white light from your crown to your feet just in case any negative emotional or physical vibrations have been picked up during the healing. Any crystals used should be soaked in sea salt.

It is recommended that you talk with your partner about what you both have experienced. Through this sharing, both of you will have a better understanding of how crystal healing works.

Self-Healing

If doing a self-healing, the crystal formations by themselves will provide you with adequate healing vibrations. They will draw out and add the necessary energy to any problem areas within the subtle bodies.

Healing works with the intervention of human hands, which increases electromagnetic stimulation and thereby directs the crystal flow. This additional power causes a dynamic exchange system to occur. If you are in the position to have someone to work with, experiment and enjoy the benefits of the next chapter's healing arrangements.

▲

10

Crystal Healing Arrangements

Crystals, when properly placed on and around our body, create a powerful magnetic field of energy. By using these vibrations, any negativity that has crystallized in our physical, etheric, emotional, and/or mental bodies can be released. The arrangements in this chapter are based on quartz crystals alleviating these imperfections. The benefits of releasing any unneeded energies from our subtle bodies are that the soul will have freer conscious expression and the body will be able to tune into finer and finer degrees of Ascension.

The following healing layouts include a Subtle Body Cleanse, Chakra Balancing, Soul Connection, and Ascension Connection. These arrangements do not require the healer to physically lay hands on the body. Instead, the hands are used to smooth out and rearrange the etheric webbing. This is done through the healer's channeled energies interacting with the vibrations emitted from the crystals. Some of the healings can be used on yourself, while others require a partner (this will be indicated in each layout).

Healing Arrangement 1
Subtle Body Cleanse

This layout is to be used for an overall emotional, mental, and physical healing. The crystal pattern will induce a gentle flow of vibrations. It is a safe introduction to healing, allowing you or your partner to become accustomed to the magnetic energies created when electromagnetic forces come in contact with human energy fields.

The healer must carefully watch for any reactions from the partner. It is possible that physical pain and emotional reactions may be intensified. The mind and body are giving up old, negative programming and allowing new, harmonizing vibrations to flow in.

This arrangement requires twelve single point crystals and a generator. It may be self-administered or done with a partner. Playing New Age music is helpful to put both (or one of you) into a more receptive state. If self-healing, lie flat on your back, face up. The arms are placed down at the sides while you are lying on the floor, bed, or healing table. If healing with a partner, have the one to be healed assume this position. All crystals need to point up toward the head to allow an energy flow from the feet to the crown. The crystals are placed approximately six inches away from the body. The placement is as follows:

- One above the center of the head
- One below the feet, lined up
  with the head crystal
- One beside the left shoulder
- One beside the right shoulder
- One at the right elbow
- One at the left elbow
- One at the right wrist
- One at the left wrist
- One at the right knee
- One at the left knee
- One at the right ankle
- One at the left ankle

Its shape will look more like an oval around the body (see diagram on page 110).

✦ Step One

- Hold the generator's apex, point down, a few inches away from the layout. If self-healing, stand (or sit) inside the configuration and begin to link the head crystal to the rest of the eleven crystals by directing the energy

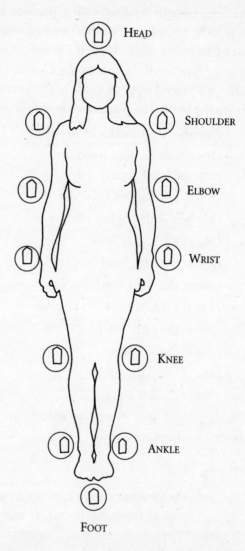

HEAD

SHOULDER

ELBOW

WRIST

KNEE

ANKLE

FOOT

✦ *Subtle Body Cleanse Layout.* The positions of the circled crystals in the layout are from Dr. Frank Alper's 3-volume study *Exploring Atlantis* (Phoenix, AZ: Arizona Metaphysical Society, 1982). Used by permission.

flow in a clockwise direction. Repeat the circuit a few more times until you feel a linkage has been made. Mentally try to visualize the circle of energy flowing as the generator is rotated. If healing a partner, from a position outside the oval repeat the same process with that person lying in the configuration.

✦ Step Two

- Set the generator aside. If healing yourself, lie down, drift into a meditative state, and mentally direct the flow of energy around and over your body.

- With a partner, extend your hands, palms down, over the third eye area as explained in Chapter 9, pages 98–101. The hands should be about four to six inches away from the body. Wait for the start of a connection to your partner's body.

- Next, move your hands to the solar plexus area. With palms down, concentrate on feeling the buildup of energy. Your palms may start to tingle or you may feel heat. If no sensations are felt, you are just not conscious of the energies. Be assured, they are there.

✦ Step Three

- Slowly move your hands over the body by walking around the layout to ensure all areas receive energy. Try experimenting with different hand movements and their position level over the body. Be guided and trust the channeled forces that are flowing through your crown chakra.

✦ Step Four

- Remove your hands after the energy field has evened out.
- Inquire as to how your partner is feeling. If all is positive, leave your partner in the arrangement for ten minutes.

✦ Step Five

- Remove the crystals and soak in a sea salt solution.
- Leave your partner to rest for a few more minutes.

The Subtle Body Cleanse may be repeated in about a week's time. The length of healing may be increased to twenty minutes. Any side effects experienced either when in the crystals or after treatment are indicative that the healing was beneficial. Releasing is expected. It is part of our development process. The spiritual and/or physical self is adjusting to incorporate the harmonious vibrations of crystals. Please give the mind and body time to adjust!

The above layout can also be done with double terminated quartz. Their use is definitely **not** recommended for a first-time healing, as the energy may be too powerful, causing adverse effects for someone not used to crystal energies. Temporary chills, heat, tingles, headaches, or sensations of disorientation could possibly occur.

Healing Arrangement 2
Chakra Balancing

The Subtle Body arrangement can be combined with seven more crystals, which are placed over the physical chakras to create a chakra balancing layout. This type of layout will assist in balancing and removing blockages in the chakras, helping you gain more access to soul energies. The quartz directly laid on the body will create a directed flow of energy from the feet straight up the center of the body and out the crown. Those around the outside form a complete energy circuit, holding and containing the intermingling vibrations of body and quartz energies.

A variation to this layout can be done if only one or two chakras are blocked by using a crystal (or crystals) over that area. For example, if the heart center is unopened, then use the oval of twelve crystals with one single crystal placed point up over this center. If the throat and third eye appear to not be functioning to your satisfaction, then each center would require a crystal along with the outside twelve crystals.

To do this arrangement, nineteen single point crystals and a generator are needed. It is slightly

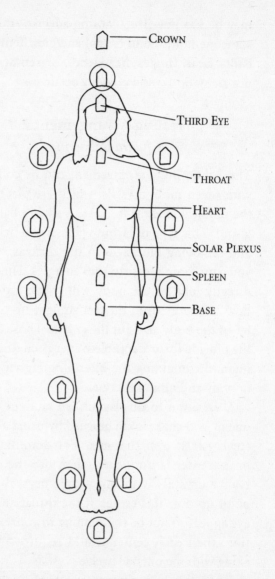

Chakra Balancing Layout. The positions of the circled crystals in the layout are from Dr. Frank Alper's 3-volume study *Exploring Atlantis* (Phoenix, AZ: Arizona Metaphysical Society, 1982). Used by permission.

awkward to set this up for yourself, but with some juggling it can be done. The instructions below are for a partner healing.

✦ Step One

- Follow the instructions as given in Arrangement 1 for placing the crystals around the body.
- Before linking their energies, place seven small crystals over each of the chakras. All points need to be directed up toward the head. It can be difficult to place a crystal on the crown chakra. Use a small book between the head crystal of the initial twelve crystals and your actual hair. Place the crystal on the book so that its base is just touching the center of your head.

The rest of the crystals are placed as follows:

- One on the base
- One over the spleen
- One on the solar plexus
- One on the heart
- One on the throat
- One on the third eye

(See diagram on page 114)

✦ Step Two

- Activate the outside twelve with the generator crystal.
- Run the generator from the feet straight up the center of the body over the chakra crystals to the head quartz.

- Link the energies with the generator down from the head along the chakra crystals to the foot quartz.
- Repeat this up-and-down connection six times.

✦ **Step Three**

- Place the generator aside. Use your hands to evenly distribute the energies.
- If your partner is comfortable, leave him or her for ten to fifteen minutes.

✦ **Step Four**

- Gently remove the stones, starting at the base, while informing your partner to mentally close up the chakra centers. To reinforce this, you can place your index finger over each center.
- Remove the outside twelve crystals and soak them all.

Healing Arrangement 3
Soul Connection

This configuration can be used when a person is having difficulty getting in touch with the higher self or soul. Meditation may be unrewarding, colors are not being seen, symbols are not appearing or messages are not being received from the soul. This layout can also be used when you feel you are ready to reach into the unlimited energies of Ascension.

To help speed up the connection of soul and Ascension, the energy needs to be pushed up from the feet and out through the head. Nineteen crystals plus a generator are needed to trigger this release. This layout cannot be self-administered.

✦ Step One

- Place the twelve crystals around the body as described in Arrangement 1, page 109.

✦ Step Two

- Place five single points, point up, evenly distributed between the foot crystal and base chakra (see diagram on page 118).
- Place the remaining two crystals point up between the head of your partner and the head crystal of the outside twelve crystals. All should be in an even line.

✦ Step Three

- Connect the outside energies.
- Using the generator, start linking from the foot crystal up the five crystals between the legs. Keep the energy flowing up the center of the body to the two head crystals and to the outside head quartz.
- Repeat this linkage six more times from the foot to the crown.

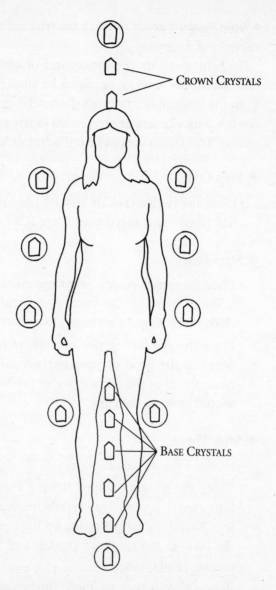

CROWN CRYSTALS

BASE CRYSTALS

✦ *Soul Connection Layout.* The positions of the circled crystals in the layout are from Dr. Frank Alper's 3-volume study *Exploring Atlantis* (Phoenix, AZ: Arizona Metaphysical Society, 1982). Used by permission.

✦ Step Four

• Place the generator aside.

• Allow this energy to flow for fifteen minutes.

✦ Step Five

• Remove the crystals and have your partner drift into a meditative state while still lying down. If there is no improvement with inner visions or a sense of connectedness, repeat this healing arrangement.

• Soak the quartz.

Healing Arrangement 4
Ascension Connection

To further connect the higher spiritual aspects of the self, a healing arrangement can be performed using the Subtle Body layout and a small cluster of crystal. This can be done on yourself or with a partner. The person needs to allow the state of meditation to occur while in this crystal arrangement.

The Ascension Connection will draw in more Ascension energies to your consciousness by contact with the golden ray. The crystal will act as a beacon to draw the higher vibrations into your third eye chakra. Symbols and pictures can appear that will be keys to helping you with your spiritual development (see diagram on page 120).

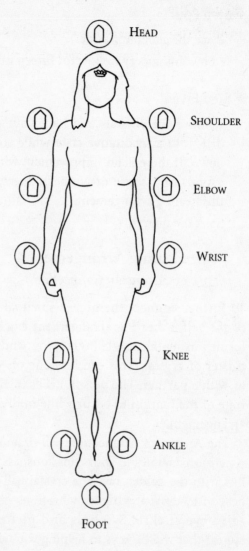

HEAD

SHOULDER

ELBOW

WRIST

KNEE

ANKLE

FOOT

◆ *Ascension Connection Layout.* The positions of the circled crystals in the layout are from Dr. Frank Alper's 3-volume study *Exploring Atlantis* (Phoenix, AZ: Arizona Metaphysical Society, 1982). Used by permission.

✦ Step One

- Place the twelve crystals around the body.
- Use the generator to ignite the energy field.

✦ Step Two

- Place the cluster, points up, directly on the third eye center.

✦ Step Three

- Allow yourself (or the person being healed) to drift into an altered state of awareness while concentrating on the stone over the sixth center.
- Flow with the energies.

✦ Step Four

- Remove and cleanse the crystals.

This configuration may be repeated as often as desired, assuming you or the other person has been exposed to the energies of the previous arrangements.

As a closing note, be guided by the higher self when choosing arrangements for yourself or a partner. Any crystal healing will instill a sense of peaceful bliss, but the right layout can start working on specific problems and blockages. It has taken us several years to build up scars in our aura. It will take more than one treatment to release them. By adding color, gemstones, and sound vibrations, healings can be more enhanced, thereby assisting our ultimate goal of connecting to higher Ascension vibrations.

▲

II

Healing with the Language of Color

The language of color is all around us. Everywhere the eyes look, varying shades and hues are registered within our minds. The seven basic rays have a subtly profound effect on our emotional and physical states.

Individual color choices for rooms, furniture, clothes, and paintings can be indicative of a mood our subconscious wishes to create for healing purposes. If we are depressed, then bright, cheerful clothing in oranges and yellows may be chosen to uplift our spirits. If a peaceful ambiance is desired, we may be attracted to decorate a room in soft hues of blue. If we want love vibrations to be drawn to us, we might wear a rose-colored necklace.

The reasons we are subconsciously drawn to a particular color can be very revealing. Try a simple

123

test. Close your eyes, go within and search for the internal motives of why you chose the shades of clothing you are wearing right now. Through this awareness, you can be consciously alerted to your current state of emotions. A suggested exercise in the morning is to let the inner self reach for a color of clothing. This is done by letting the left hand do the selecting. Because of its connection to the right hemisphere of the brain, it will be a true reflection of what the subconscious self needs.

There is a purer form of color healing found in Nature. Her colors surround and envelop our aura with life-filling energies. When we are in a natural setting, we pick up on the delightful vibrations of life and feel part of that force, whether it be a forest, waterfall, lake, beach, or tree. We experience a rejuvenation after spending time in Nature, away from our congested cities. Our entire being becomes recharged with renewed vitality from the healing rays emitted from the blues of the sky, greens of the trees, and browns of the earth.

Most of us are unable to regularly escape to the trees and fields, but we can obtain similar healing benefits through using colored quartz and gemstones.

Color properties given in Chapter 4 and Chapter 7 describe the effects of colored minerals on our emotional and physical well-being. Also explained was that colored vibrations enter our subtle bodies through the chakras. This means that colored healing adds energy to our aura for balancing and releasing a physical, emotional, or mental condition.

The information on page 126 is designed to help the healer facilitate changes in the subtle bodies by using quartz and gemstone layouts. The healing arrangements are for smoky quartz, amethyst, rose quartz, citrine, and various gemstones. The properties of gemstones were given in Chapter 7 and those of colored quartz are given below, with suggested healing layouts.

Any of the colored quartz above can be worn on the body as jewelry. If you wish to work directly on a problem area, use a bandage or tape a small stone over that area. Remove it when you feel its energies have helped.

Smoky Quartz Layout

Some people may shy away from smoky quartz because of the black shading. Its darkness is in no way indicative of negativity. This crystal's energies can help to release anger, resentment, and depression.

Smoky quartz can be exchanged for the clear foot crystal in the healing pattern of twelve crystals. Or, it can be placed directly over the base chakra, surrounded by the clear pattern. In either

GEMSTONES AND THEIR SPIRITUAL PROPERTIES

Type	Color	Spiritual Properties
smoky	black, grey to brown shades	• grounding force to physical world • alleviates depression • protects against psychic attacks • revitalizes energy
amethyst	deep purple to pale violet	• facilitates deep, meaningful meditations • opens third eye to receiving information from soul and universal thoughts • raises up heavy physical vibrations into spiritual aspects
rose	pinkish red to white	• opens heart chakra to giving and receiving love vibrations • instills peacefulness in times of adversity • removes negativity from the aura
citrine	goldish yellow to light brown	• opens solar plexus center • invokes personal power • removes self-doubts • promotes creative and intellectual endeavors

position, the conditions listed above can be worked on. The energy connection and healing process is done in the same way as clear quartz.

Amethyst Layout

To draw spiritual energies into the aura from higher vibrations, the pattern of twelve crystals can be replaced with amethyst points. This entire violet layout is especially beneficial for a person who feels too grounded to the third dimension and wishes more spiritual enhancement.

An amethyst point or small cluster can be exchanged for clear quartz by placing it directly over the third eye in the Chakra Balancing layout.

Rose Quartz Layout

Rose or pink quartz is a natural choice to open the heart center. A chunk, small cluster, or point is laid directly on this chakra in the Chakra Balancing layout.

An outside energy force field can be erected around the body using twelve rose quartz. Warm, calming, soothing, pink pastel vibrations will gently filter into the aura causing us to feel at peace with all aspects of life. This pink light also connects to the master level of Ascension, bringing knowledge and enlightenment into our being.

Citrine Layout

This stone activates the solar plexus. Unlimited benefits can be obtained by placing citrine over this chakra within a pattern of twelve crystals.

Citrine is a powerful stone to help us be more assertive. For example, there is often a conflict within women about assuming power in the business world. To balance love together with personal power, place a pink quartz over the heart chakra and citrine on the solar plexus within the pattern of twelve crystals. The colored quartz will help to balance the energies of love and power.

These uses are just a few suggestions to introduce you to colored quartz energies. The variations for healing layouts are numerous. As you become more energized by crystals, you will intuitively discover the numerous ways they are here to serve us.

Gemstone and Quartz Healing Patterns

Colored healing can be a combination of gemstones and clear quartz. The stones can be laid directly on the body within a pattern of twelve crystals. The outside quartz acts as a container for the energies of the subtle bodies, making it easier for the healer to work with a portion of the aura. The electrons within our bodies become magnetized or energized with color. The body's energy absorbs and then transforms the colors into a healing language. If a person has a blocked throat center, a blue stone such as lapis can be put over this chakra while the person is inside the pattern of twelve clear quartz. The healing would be performed in the usual manner of spreading the energies, using a generator, et cetera.

For a self-healing, simply place the gemstone over the problem area as you are lying down in the pattern (a referral to Chapter 7 might be helpful for placing the appropriate stone on the right center).

Chakra Layout

This arrangement requires twelve clear single points, seven gemstones, and a generator. After the person is lying with the Subtle Body pattern, a red stone, such as a garnet or a ruby, is placed on the base chakra. An orange crystal, such as carnelian, is centered over the spleen. A yellow topaz goes on the solar plexus, malachite or any green mineral is put on the heart chakra, blue adventurine or lapis on the throat, sodalite or another indigo shade at the third eye and fluorite at the crown.

This layout can be used for self or partner healing following the usual directions of connecting the outside energies and then running

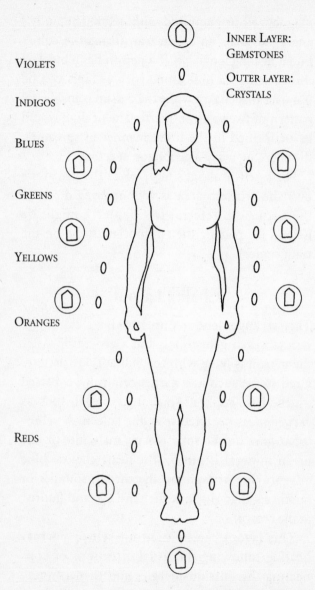

INNER LAYER:
GEMSTONES

OUTER LAYER:
CRYSTALS

VIOLETS

INDIGOS

BLUES

GREENS

YELLOWS

ORANGES

REDS

✦ *Aura Coloring Layout.* The positions of the circled crystals in the layout are from Dr. Frank Alper's 3-volume study *Exploring Atlantis* (Phoenix, AZ: Arizona Metaphysical Society, 1982). Used by permission.

the generator up and down the stones, which lie
in a straight line up the center of the body. The
actual physical sensations may not be as intense
as when clear quartz points were on the body, but
the chakras are receiving color vibrations for balancing and opening.

Aura Coloring Layout

Gemstones make an excellent seal of protection
for the etheric body. Their energies may be locked
into the auric field by using a variety of colored
stones within a pattern of twelve clear points. The
outside energies will fill in and compensate for
any energy imperfections in this layout.

A minimum of ten tumbled stones are needed.
Ideally, the colors should include the seven basic
chakra shades. A generator and twelve clear crystals are also required.

The purpose of this layout is to create two separate circles of energy. One is four inches at the
etheric level and the other is farther away at the
emotional or mental level. The outside circle
forms a magnetic field to amplify and contain the
colors emitted from the inner circle of stones.
This double layout can be done before you go
into any situation where you know a lot of negativity will be encountered, such as a hospital,
court of law, or stressful business meeting.
Potential damage to the aura can be prevented.
Or, this layout can be used as an overall energy
booster to increase your spiritual and physical

well-being. It can be done on a partner or as a
self-healing.

✦ Step One

- Have your partner lie, back down, on the
  floor.
- Begin to place the gemstones approximately
  four inches away around the body in a fairly
  uniform, evenly-spaced manner. The reds
  will go around the feet and legs, the oranges
  at the sides in the area of the spleen, yellows
  at the solar plexus, and so on. The lightest
  spiritual colors go around the crown. This
  completes the inner circle (see diagram on
  page 130).
- If self-healing, place the stones on the floor in
  their approximate position before stepping
  inside the layout.

✦ Step Two

- Place twelve clear quartz, points directed
  upward, about six inches away from the gemstones. This completes the outer circle.

✦ Step Three

- Using a generator, connect all the stones in
  the inner circle in a clockwise direction for
  one circuit.
- Connect the crystals in the outside circle for
  three to six rotations until you feel the energy
  linkage has been made.

✦ Step Four

- Leave the person (or yourself) to lie in a semimeditative state for twenty minutes. Do not distribute the magnetic fields with your hands. Let the crystals do the work of filling in the missing color vibrations within the auric field.

✦ Step Five

- Remove and cleanse all the stones.

The after-effects of this healing are sensations of peaceful harmony with the soul and a calmness that allows you to face any adversity with strength and determination.

Colored Hands

An alternative to using colored quartz or gemstones for healing is to color clear quartz with your own mental thoughts. This method can be used for crystals placed directly on or around the body.

To instill color, project the shade first onto your mind's screen by closing your eyes. Imagine that ray filling up your entire being and then shoot this color out through your hands. Imagine two green or pink spots (or whatever color feels right for the healing) in the palms of your hands. See the color as two brilliant crystals burning in your palms. Now, as if you were painting, brush the color on to smooth in and cover up the aura of the one being treated. You are blanketing the etheric body in color.

This type of colored hands healing is very effective, as the color can be altered to suit the situation. For instance, the healing might begin with green for an overall physical treatment, then switch to indigo to replenish or add spiritual vibrations. Experiment with this type of mind healing and keep practicing it until you feel confident that you are sending colors into the other person's energy fields.

New Age healers are just beginning to tap into the language of color for healing the mind, body, and soul. As the consciousness of this planet keeps ascending, we will be able to recall the lost art of using color.

▲

12

The Sound of Music

Sound is a vibrational force perpetrating the energy fields of all matter. Each and every sound that reaches our ears triggers a spontaneous emotional and/or physical response. Most of us jump when an unexpected, loud noise is heard. The alarm clock jolts us awake from a deep sleep. Chalk scraped across the blackboard sends shivers up our spines. A crying child alerts us that help is needed. Sirens blaring in the street warn drivers to pull over. A lover's voice can fill a beloved with warmth.

Other life forms respond to sounds that are often inaudible to us. A high-pitched whistle signals a dog that his master is calling. Fish and underwater mammals are sensitive to low, droning noises.

Crystals and gemstones resonate when sounds are synonymous with their molecular rate of vibration. Glass shatters if a note is struck above its vibrational frequency level.

When the vibrational intensity of sounds increases, it is transformed into music. This energy acceleration can be irritating noise or beautiful harmony, depending on our personal preferences.

When varying tones are sung or played in a melodic, rhythmic order, sound becomes music to the ears. It plays on the emotional, mental, and physical conditions of the listener or singer. When a mother softly coos a lullaby, she is using her voice to relax her child's mind and body. Conversely, booming or harsh music would jar the child into an alert state. When some of us listen to classical masterpieces composed by Bach or Mozart, the mathematical precision of their notes evoke varying responses. Our energy level can increase, the mind can become more alert, and suppressed emotions may surface. When we become one, flowing with the music, our current state of consciousness is altered.

Sound need not only be external. Inner music can be created by singing and chanting. These self-generated internal vibrations are not only healing but create a powerful bond between the people who are performing together. To religious congregations, classmates, teammates, club members, healing circles and cults, any vocal expression in the form of harmony pulls all the group's energies together.

Through song, a heightened sense of comradeship and awareness is created, and the vibrations of the participants are intermingled and raised into higher realms. The healing powers that are tapped into are drawn into the group, benefiting them as a whole and individually.

Music and certain sounds, whether external or self-induced, can be used as healing tools to rearrange and balance our body's chakras. Each organ, chakra, and subtle body resonates, vibrates, and harmonizes with the sound of music.

To assist us in becoming more attuned with ourselves, others, Ascension energies, crystals, and our soul, the application of vocal and instrumental sound is introduced in this chapter. The healing vibrations of music can be used to further advance us along the path to higher awareness.

Colored Notes

Sound can be applied as a healing and consciousness-raising tool by using the musical scale. Each of its notes can be assigned one of the seven color vibrations, which corresponds to a physical chakra. The chart on page 138 illustrates the note, color, chakra, and musical syllable on a piano keyboard.

When healing any physical or emotional problems related to the base chakra, in referencing the chart the note G, corresponding to the color red, would be used. It could be played or sung as *fa*. To work on the heart center, the green of C (*doh*) is sounded. If creativity needs to be stimulated, B (*la*) assigned to the yellow of the solar plexus, would be used. Playing E (*me*) will exercise the intuitive capacity of the third eye, and so on throughout the scale.

Each half note also elicits a healing response. For instance, if C sharp was played, this half note will open the flow between the heart and throat chakra. Reversed, D flat will have the same effect. Or, if your throat center is blocked, the D flat or C sharp would connect its energies down to the heart center, enabling this center to open up.

NOTE	COLOR	CHAKRA	SYLLABLE
C	green	heart	doh
D	blue	throat	ray
E	indigo	third eye	me
F	violet	crown	soh
G	red	base	fa
A	orange	spleen	la
B	yellow	solar plexus	te

KEYBOARD

The notes can be sounded while meditating or in crystal healing arrangements. A suggestion is to record a series of sustained Cs, Ds, Es, et cetera, for at least one minute each and then replay them as needed. Or, singing these notes may be done. Try experimenting with triads, chords, sharps, flats, and other arrangements to discover what note or notes have an effect on your chakras.

Soul Note

One of the first steps in using music for personal healing and heightening awareness is to find your soul note. Each of us has a sound that our soul resonates with. When this tone is reproduced, a harmonious resonance is created, causing energy to be transferred from the soul to the physical body. Ascension vibrations are then linked to our energy fields. Not only does this sound empower us for healing work, but we have a deeper insight into universal truths.

One way to discover your soul note is to sound each note within the scale as suggested above. Listen to the sustained notes while meditating. This experience can be heightened while done within the pattern of twelve crystals. The soul sound will be recognized as a feeling of coming home or a return to something loving and famil-iar. Physical reactions can be heat, chills, tingles, or tears of joy. However your personal note is found, it should be recorded in sustained versions for use during healing and meditation.

Chanting

An alternative to using a musical instrument is to chant the soul vibration. Chanting is done by using vowels and consonants together and singing them repeatedly on the same note. It stimulates the physical body and strengthens the auric field to intensify your energy for higher light work.

The universal healing sound is the chanted *om* of middle C. Associated with the color green, the *om* is used for overall healing. It centers awareness on the heart chakra. When several people chant together, the resonance fills each person with a complete oneness with self, others, and the energies of Ascension.

Instructions for chanting are:

1) Loosen all restrictive clothing.

2) Stand with your legs slightly parted. Close your eyes for better concentration.

3) Open your chakras up to the twelfth level.

4) Start to breathe from the diaphragm, inhaling and exhaling in a rhythmic count. Open your mouth and relax the jaw.

5) Draw energy up from the feet through the base, spleen, solar plexus, and heart, and release it through the throat by chanting the word *om* as middle C. As its power leaves the throat, focus your attention on the upper chakras by mentally envisioning them opening to their maximum.

6) Sustain the *om* until all the air is released from the body.

7) Repeat this process several times until you feel your entire body resonating with the sound.

Chanting can be done before a healing or a meditation to increase your connection to higher vibrations.

Chanting Your Soul Note

After you feel adept at chanting middle C, you are ready to tune in to your soul note. Try chanting the word *om* to each note of the scale. You will recognize your personal note by the intensity of any physical or emotional responses. You may wish to experiment with other vowel and consonant combinations such as *hum, lah,* or *may,* or chants will be intuitively given to you.

Chanting your soul's note is extremely powerful while you are in a crystal arrangement. Sing it three or more times and then allow the crystals to work on and around your body.

Some light workers can discover the soul note of others by laying their hands over the person's heart chakra and hearing it as sound. If the healer then chants this note while healing, the energy is greatly increased.

When sound is coupled with crystal energy, a dynamic healing team occurs. We are just on the threshold of tapping into the infinite possibilities of this powerful energy.

The practical applications of meditation, healing, color, and sound have been presented here to hopefully entice healers, light workers, and crystal initiates to begin their own personal research and experimentation. Every person will develop individual ways of interpreting and applying crystal energies. There is no one correct way and no one source of information.

Always be guided by your inner voice as to what is best for you, and never lose sight of the fact that crystals are in our lives for the betterment of humankind and of Earth.

▲

Unlimitedness

SECTION IV

13

Programming
for Prosperity

Thoughts are vibrational energies existing both in our mind and in the universe. They can be our best friends or our worst enemies. If we think we are loving, beautiful, healthy, creative, and intelligent, these vibrations are projected to other people and attract like energies from the universe. On the other hand, if we believe we are unloved, unattractive, unhealthy, lacking intelligence, and we harbor a host of other self-defeating judgments, not only do others perceive us in these ways but we also invite the negative aspects of universal thought back to us. Thoughts, both positive and negative, are reflected in every aspect of our lives. What we think, we are.

Universal vibrations are energies floating outside our auras that contain thoughts emitted from all life forms. These energies hold positive and negative vibrations that can be repelled by or attracted into our personal energy fields. This filtering process is dependent on the status of our thoughts. If we hold any self-demeaning attitudes, negative people and circumstances are drawn into our lives. If health, happiness, and prosperity are part of us, then these signals are sent out to attract similar, positive vibrations.

Thoughts also exist inside our aura. As explained in Chapter 2, they originate in the mental body. Depending on their intensity, these thoughts can filter into the emotional, etheric, and physical selves. If the subconscious and conscious are in agreement with the thought of perfect health, our emotions reflect this positive energy. More energy is attracted from the universe, which then causes the body to respond with glowing vitality.

There is another type of thought called "collective consciousness." This term refers to ideas and thought forms that are available for us to link up with. These are where the ideas for new technology, innovative enterprises, and creativity originate. It is quite common for two people in different parts of the world to have a similar idea at the same time. If they choose to bring the idea into reality, each will interpret it in their own unique way, but the basic concepts will be similar. They both have tapped into collective consciousness.

The mind is constantly filled with thoughts from within and without. Some internal thoughts can be most annoying when they cannot be shut off, especially when we are trying to fall asleep or meditate. We think about the day's events, things we have not done, and other nagging thoughts. When we bring any thought from any of the three origins into the third dimension and actually carry it out, it is cleared from our energy. Writing that letter, leaving the unhealthy relationship, or creating a new art form brings thoughts into being. We can change our lives for the better by making the right kinds of thoughts into reality and shutting off those that are of a negative nature.

The Power of Thought

One internal and external thought we should program ourselves to manifest is prosperity. Prosperity means different things to each of us. For some it could mean material wealth, while to others it could mean Ascension enlightenment. We each need to answer what it means to us before programming for prosperity. We all have the capability to have abundance in our lives, to fulfill dreams and needs by making the right thoughts into reality. Prosperity can be put to work in finding a job, a special someone, healing ourself and others, promoting a creative enterprise, or making money.

In order to bring prosperity into being, a special mental and spiritual place of thinking has to be reached. There are four steps to abundance:

1) Changing negative thinking

2) Having inner faith

3) Performing creative visualization
   with crystals

4) Putting effort into making thoughts a reality

✦ Changing Negative Thinking

The first step in manifesting prosperity is being aware of our thinking process. If we have negative thoughts, whether from universal vibrations or our internal thoughts, reprogramming needs to be done.

We need to stop looking outside ourselves and blaming others for our problems. We must truly look within and examine whether we are harboring self-defeating thoughts. Do we feel unworthy of receiving praise? Do we feel other people are more fortunate than we are? Are we afraid of being alone? These thoughts all need to be released. The crystal meditations and healings will already have brought some of the negative aspects of the personality and ego to surface. Now is the time for self-examination and reprogramming.

The knowledge that we have the capability to better ourselves simply by the thinking process is present for anyone pursuing Ascension.

✦ Having Inner Faith

The second step to bring prosperity into being is having the inner belief, faith, and understanding that the universe always provides.

As children, we believed all things were possible. Perhaps as a young adult all your efforts were put into studying to become an engineer, teacher, doctor, designer, or whatever you wanted to be. It did come about because you believed in your abilities. If there was not enough money for a university degree, you worked part-time, studied while working, or did whatever you had to do in order to fulfill your goal. Maybe you wanted to play the piano, dance, or join a sports team, so all your energies were directed into pursuing that dream. You succeeded because you believed in your own capabilities and you had the inner faith that it could be done.

In order to have the universe work with us, we must believe in our own abilities. We want to attract positive, rewarding universal vibrations.

We all have varying degrees of faith. These convictions are not always in things we can see. We may have faith in a religion, an herbal remedy, a crystal energy, or higher guidance. We might have the belief that we are pursuing the path to Ascension, reading the right books, making the right friends, and learning from the right teachers. We have a need and the belief that the universe will guide us to fulfill it.

✦ Creative Visualization

The next step involves taking an idea, then making it real by seeing it as already happening. We need to work on what is desired rather than the way things are. This means if you are unemployed, you don't concentrate on being unemployed. Instead, see yourself, right this minute, behind the desk, sitting in your chair within the walls of the company you want to work for. Visualize that paycheck in your hands. See yourself smiling and at peace. Create the precise scenario for prosperity instead of dwelling on the circumstances you are in already. If a perfect love relationship is desired, see you and that special someone sharing projects, making love, on vacation, and being together as two people who totally enjoy each other's company.

✦ Making It a Reality

The final step is to put the effort into making prosperity a reality.

Chapter 6, *Preparing to Use Crystals,* explains how to project mental thoughts into quartz. The projection is always on the final outcome. For instance, if you need to be healed of a particular emotional or physical problem, the programmed thought is a picture of you in perfect health, smiling and enjoying life to the fullest. The same principle applies to draw prosperity. After carefully thinking about what you want, choose a crystal to work with. It may be a single point, cluster, or double terminated quartz. Chunks are not recommended as they have no terminations to spiral the thought into the universe.

If you are uncertain about which crystal to use for a prosperity projection, drop into a meditative state, hold the quartz, and ask for inner guidance and assistance from the higher levels of the universe. If nothing is felt or sensed, this is an indication that the crystal is not the right one. Your body may respond with tiny tingles, surges of energy, or a verbal confirmation may be heard with the inner senses alerting you that this is the correct crystal.

Crystal Programming

The following steps will help you in programming your prosperity thought into the crystal:

1) Sit in a comfortable position with feet flat on the floor.

2) Close your eyes and open all twelve chakras.

3) Hold the crystal in both hands to ensure a complete energy circuit. Place the stone up to the third eye. If it is a single point, place the base against your skin. If you are using a cluster, the points need to be directed away from your face. If it is a double termination, either point can be against this chakra.

4) You are going to verbally voice your prosperity program. The sound of your words will reinforce the thought. A suggestion for doing this is the following:

> I call on the golden light from the creator (I Am) level of Ascension. I invoke the energies of Mother Earth to pour up through my body. I request that I be connected with the energy of this crystal to assist me in projecting my thoughts into the universal vibrations. I ask that *(insert your thought here)* be drawn into my auric field and manifest for me.

5) Close your chakras. Place the crystal in sunlight for further energizing and amplification of the program.

6) The thought may be projected three more times if you feel it is necessary.

You must be extremely careful to project positive thoughts. If any self-doubts are harbored about what is being requested, you can draw negative universal vibrations into your personal energy fields. Be clear in what you ask.

Once the thought of working and receiving a paycheck has been put into a crystal, guidance will be received. You will be in the right place at the right time or news will somehow reach you about a job. No matter what you have programmed for, be assured you will be guided to connect to the necessary circumstances and make the manifestation.

Another way to increase the projection of prosperity is to send out the thought through a crystal with the addition of color. When you are sending out thoughts for manifestation, send them out with a corresponding color (refer to Chapter 4 on the twelve colors related to the chakras for help). For example, if you wish to be connected to the mental level of consciousness to write a book or create a painting, then you would send this thought through the crystal along with the color of aquamarine. If you are requesting prosperity in a career, send out the mental thought with the color of yellow from the solar plexus center. If you wish to have love in your life, send the mental program with green from the heart center. The possibilities are unlimited.

As we advance our consciousness, we must
never underestimate the power of thought. We
are now more attuned with universal vibrations
and collective consciousness than ever before. Let
these energies work with us, helping us to be
prosperous in everything we do. As a final note,
time limitations must never be put on manifesting abundance. If faith is lost, this type of thinking will cancel out the projection. What we sow,
we reap.

▲

14

Ascension
Tools

Along with using the Ascension-raising vibrations of quartz for programming prosperity,
heightening meditation, and for healing layouts,
their energies can be put to practical, everyday use.
These light tools can enhance dream recall, ener-
gize a room, protect our car, assist pets and children, and form telepathic links with other people.
There is no limit to the diversity of crystals.

Dreams

When a personal crystal becomes attuned to our
vibrations, it guides and directs our subconscious
and conscious thoughts. Therefore, it is only
natural to use its attributes during the sleep state.
By instilling a dream recall or dream guidance
program into a crystal, night journeys will slowly
be remembered. If an urgent problem requires a

solution or a decision, this programmed crystal will help put us in touch with the soul's answer.

To recall dreams, program your crystal with the image of yourself awakening in the morning and reviewing your night visions. Place the quartz on its side, point up, under your pillow before sleeping. Before getting out of bed in the morning, reach under your pillow and hold the crystal in the left hand. Request that significant messages be revealed to you. If no images immediately surface, go about your day. Something will trigger a response to your request. It is then up to you to decipher what the dreams mean.

Dreams are not always easy to discern. They are often misty blurs of seemingly nonsensical information. Our teachers, guides, and soul rarely communicate in actual words. If we wish to derive full benefits from our nightly journeys, these messages need further interpretation upon awakening. It is up to us to decide whether the dreams were of future events, past life information, or solutions to current problems. We need to translate these often cryptic symbols into a language we can understand and take direction from.

Dreams related to the prediction of forthcoming events are meant to alert and prepare us. They can usually be taken literally, with some alterations. The imagery can be as simple as an upcoming meeting with an old friend or as complex as an emotionally disruptive situation.

Past life information may come through to help us understand why we are in certain predicaments and the reasons for significant relationships. This type of dreaming usually depicts us in actual scenes from past times. It we are given the dream information of being in a position of power such as a priestess, pharaoh, witch, or warrior, the message is relayed to our consciousness that our soul is more knowing and self-assured than our personality realizes. This type of dream is telling us that we have the inner strength to work through a difficult time in our lives.

Symbolic dreams are the hardest to decode. Encountering a snake can mean the personality is up against some type of fearful situation. Images of death can be a rebirth experience or the end of a relationship. Rarely are the outcomes to be taken literally. There are several books, workshops, and therapists now that help us decipher what dreams actually mean. Over a period of time, we will be able to decode our information on our own. The soul will be able to give us the proper interpretation. If the answer is not readily available to the satisfaction of our consciousness, then we need to let it go for the time being. Later, it will fall into place. Often only segments of dreams will be recalled. This is to entice us to go and discover the unwritten message from within.

Crystals will assist the conscious mind to remember and bring the dream message into third-dimensional terminology. Through dream recall, we will establish another strong communication link with our soul.

Wall of Energy

If there is a designated area within your home
where healing and meditation are done, this
room can be constantly energized by a wall of
crystals. Quartz, when programmed to remove
undesirable energies, provides a continuous light
center by cleansing, recharging, and energizing.
This formation is created by laying a number of
clear single points or double terminations on the
floor touching the walls. They need to lie on their
sides, point-to-base if single points. Space the
crystals equally around the perimeter of the
room. Use a generator to fully connect the energies on a daily basis. If a releasing of an emotional nature occurs in this area from a healing or a
meditation session, the crystals should be
removed. Soak them in a sea salt solution and
place the quartz back in position.

An alternative to an entire crystal wall is the
setting of clear quartz single points, point up, in
each of the four corners of your special room. All
should be programmed to remove negativity
from this area. The same number of crystals can
be put in the four corners of a house or an apart-
ment. If the bases do not permit them to stand
up, plant these crystals in a pot of soil (nonchem-
ical variety) with their points exposed.

Car Crystals

A single point, cluster, or double terminated
quartz can be placed in a car for protection. With

a program of seeing yourself, your passengers, and your vehicle in a bubble of white light, accidents and car trouble can be warded off. The crystal can be inserted under the floor mat, seat, or in the glove compartment. Take it out for periodic cleansing and recharging.

Pet Crystals

Because all life forms resonate together, crystals can be put in your pet's sleeping area. As with human vibrations, over a period of time the crystal will harmoniously balance any imperfections in the pet's subtle bodies. The animal will develop a more congenial disposition.

Crystals for Children

Children can also tune into higher vibrations with the help of crystals. The crystals will gently balance their spiritual and physical lives. Giving a crystal to a child affords them the opportunity to have many wonderful experiences. Because they have not yet had their imagination and spontaneity stifled, children hear, see, and extract information from crystals. As parents, we can program these stones to help remove blockages, heal emotional and physical conditions, and increase creativity and self-worthiness, as well as instill other desired characteristics. A crystal can be tucked safely under a mattress, sewn into a pillow, worn as jewelry, or used in any other sensible manner.

The sooner we educate our children to the unlimited potential of crystals and open their hearts and minds to the energies of Ascension, the better they will be able to deal with the rapid changes of this New Age.

Connecting Force

A crystal that has been worn next to the body for a minimum of two weeks and programmed with loving thoughts can be given to a friend or a loved one who is physically removed from us. This connecting force is even more powerful when both parties exchange crystals. In times of despair, loneliness, joy, or excitement, comfort can be readily obtained from just holding such a crystal. It puts both of you in a telepathic soul link. The crystal is a symbol of loving energy putting both people in touch with each other's emotional and mental conditions.

Spiritual advancement is a way of life. As we progress into higher levels of Ascension and self-realization, more and more practical applications for crystals will come to mind. The above only touched on the fringes of benefits derived from these light tools. Their potential is just as limit-less as ours.

▲

15
The Final
Transformation

As we make the transition to union with soul, we are releasing the ego's restrictive personality traits. We are aware, not only of the effort, but of the struggles involved in so doing.

When we open up to Ascension energies, a natural confrontation occurs between the fearful personality and the inner essence of soul. We often release our inner being much faster than our ego would like. As the soul is beginning to release its beautiful potential into conscious expression, personality vehemently resists. So, a struggle develops between the knowingness of soul and the uncertainty of ego/personality. There is a resistance to letting go of old programming and self-defeating concepts, and a lack of trusting in one's abilities to heal or in intuitive feelings.

The soul walks in light and beauty but is often held back from true expression by the personality unless there is a strong commitment and effort to bring it forth. By using crystal vibrations, we slowly begin to let ego be influenced by soul.

Universal Oneness

When we start to know who we really are, then the necessary changes can be made to allow our full potential to shine forth. By not harboring restrictive thoughts, not being self-centered, not judging or condemning ourselves or others, and not seeking revenge, we can take full responsibility for our lives. It is at this stage of ascending our vibrations that ego transcends into soul, and we have achieved the higher levels of Ascension. We are part of the Universal Oneness.

The creator (I Am) is in every creation. Everything comes from the Creative Source. When we learn to love and respect all life forms, then we move into a very special inner place of unconditional love and respect for all that is.

Ascension Energies

In this New Aquarian Age, we are being altered physically and spiritually by the influx of Ascension energies. We are in the process of transcending the heavy restrictions, not only of our physical bodies, but of how we relate to the three-dimensional world, by attracting higher levels of light, knowledge, and understanding. We are evolving toward the final Ascension transformation of the creator (I Am). It is from this level of Ascension that we have the possibility of altering the structure of our bodies into pure light forms. This does not entail a physical death. Instead it is a raising of the body's cellular structures into finer and finer degrees of light. In a light body we can appear in physical form whenever and wherever at will. Thoughts will instantaneously manifest. There is no limitation to creativity, healing powers, prosperity, world peace, and unconditional love. The prospects are limitless.

By consciously connecting with the Ascension vibrations, our lives have more meaning, purpose, and direction. We are strengthening our auric fields to block disease. Old, negative programming and destructive emotions are recognized, released, and replaced by positive ones. We are learning to give and receive unconditional love. Channels of communication are opening to children, family members, friends, lovers, spiritual guides, Nature, other life forms, and master levels of consciousness. We are learning to have faith in the universal flow of abundance and prosperity. We are more accepting of our chosen lessons and experiences, taking full responsibility for our own actions. We are starting to live for the moment and enjoy all that life has to offer.

We are happier, healthier, more optimistic, and reflective. Our eyes, the windows to the soul, shine with a serene knowingness. We understand and take steps to alter adversity. Our physical selves are becoming purer, stronger temples for our souls. We are becoming the best we can be. We are progressing towards integrating the vibrations of the twelfth level of Ascension. We are the creator (I Am). We no longer look at other beings as separate and removed from ourselves. No person, animal, plant, or mineral is less of a living energy than ourselves. By fully opening all our chakras and embracing our soul, we can establish an enriching rapport with all aspects of life.

Ascension energies have been channeled to Earth at a very strategic time in our lives. Because we chose to be here now, we are choosing to be the best that we can be by embracing these harmonizing vibrations. We are here to serve humankind in the highest, most beneficial way. We are the Light Workers and Children of Light. We can deal with any spiritual and physical issues using the highest level of discernment. We have faith that the Universe will provide for us. We can flow with the ebbs and flood tides of life. We have a deep commitment to our path of enlightenment and trust in our inner voice. We know who we are and that soul is here to help us achieve our goals. Collectively we are beginning to make this planet into the promised Garden of Eden.

Although crystals are Nature's gifts to assist us in consciously accomplishing the highest levels of Ascension, the ultimate responsibility falls on each individual's shoulders. With faith and the inner conviction to be the best possible expression of our souls, Ascension is part of our lives.

The sensations of unearthly energy I felt in the King's Chamber were the vibrations of Ascension. I was just at the beginning stages of understanding how Ascension could transform my life. All my experiences since that time in the Great Pyramid have been preparing me to fully embrace the energies of Ascension.

*T*ransform all that you are into light. Become a light body and experience the wonderment of the higher dimensions. You are just at the beginning stages of embracing and discovering what exactly Ascension means and how it will transform our beings in the twenty-first century . . . a new beginning.

▲

Bibliography
and
Related Readings

Alper, Frank. *Exploring Atlantis.* 3 vols. Phoenix, AZ: Arizona Metaphysical Society, 1982.

Bonewitz, Ra. *Cosmic Crystals.* Whitstable, UK: Whitstable Litho Ltd., 1983.

Bowman, Catherine. *Crystal Awareness.* St. Paul, MN: Llewellyn, 1987.

Butler, W. E. *The Aura.* Northamptonshire, UK: The Aquarian Press, 1985.

Cunningham, Scott. *Cunningham's Encyclopedia of Crystal, Gem & Metal Magic.* St. Paul, MN: Llewellyn, 1988.

DaEl. *The Crystal Book.* Sunol, CA: The Crystal Company, 1985.

David, William. *The Harmonics of Sound, Color and Vibration.* Marina del Rey, CA: DeVorss and Company, 1984.

Galde, Phyllis. *Crystal Healing: The Next Step*. St. Paul, MN: Llewellyn, 1988.

Grattan, Brian. *Mahatma I & II*. Sedona, AZ: Light Technology Publishing, 1994.

Hawken, P. *The Magic of Findhorn*. New York: Harper and Row, 1975.

Kunz, George Frederick. *The Curious Lore of Precious Stones*. New York: Dover Publications, Inc., 1971.

Leadbeater, C. W. *The Chakras*. London, UK: The Theosophical Publishing House, 1927.

Lily, John C. *Man and Dolphin*. New York: Doubleday, 1961.

Redfield, James. *The Celestine Prophecy*. Hoover, AL: Satori Publishing, 1993.

Smith, Michael. *Crystal Power*. St. Paul, MN: Llewellyn, 1985.

Stein, Diane. *The Women's Book of Healing*. St. Paul, MN: Llewellyn, 1987.

Index

169

Stay in Touch...

Llewellyn publishes hundreds of books
on your favorite subjects

On the following pages you will find listed some books now available on related subjects. Your local bookstore stocks most of these and will stock new Llewellyn titles as they become available. We urge your patronage.

Order by Phone

Call toll-free within the U.S. and Canada, 1–800–THE MOON. In Minnesota call (612) 291–1970.
We accept Visa, MasterCard, and American Express.

Order by Mail

Send the full price of your order (MN residents add 7% sales tax) in U.S. funds to:

Llewellyn Worldwide
P.O. Box 64383, Dept. K075-2
St. Paul, MN 55164–0383, U.S.A.

Postage and Handling

- ✦ $4.00 for orders $15.00 and under
- ✦ $5.00 for orders over $15.00
- ✦ No charge for orders over $100.00

We ship UPS in the continental United States. We cannot ship to P.O. boxes. Orders shipped to Alaska, Hawaii, Canada, Mexico, and Puerto Rico will be sent first class mail.

International orders: Airmail—add freight equal to price of each book to the total price of order, plus $5.00 for each non-book item (audiotapes, etc.). Surface mail—Add $1.00 per item.

Allow 4–6 weeks delivery on all orders. Postage and handling rates subject to change.

Group Discounts

We offer a 20% quantity discount to group leaders or agents. You must order a minimum of 5 copies of the same book to get our special quantity price.

Free Catalog

Get a free copy of our color catalog, *New Worlds of Mind and Spirit*. Subscribe for just $10.00 in the United States and Canada ($20.00 overseas, first class mail). Many bookstores carry *New Worlds*—ask for it!

Crystal Awareness

Catherine Bowman

For millions of years, crystals have been waiting for people to discover their wonderful powers. Today they are used in watches, computer chips and communication devices. But there is also a spiritual, holistic aspect to crystals.

Crystal Awareness will teach you everything you need to know about crystals to begin working with them. It will also help those who have been working with them to complete their knowledge. Topics include crystal forms, colored and colorless crystals, single points, clusters and double terminated crystals, crystal and human energy fields, the etheric and spiritual bodies, crystals as energy generators, crystal cleansing and programming, crystal meditation, the value of polished crystals, crystals and personal spiritual growth, crystals and chakras, how to make crystal jewelry, the uses of crystals in the future, color healing, programming crystals with color, compatible crystals and metals, and several crystal healing techniques, including the Star of David Healing.

Crystal Awareness is destined to be the guide of choice for people who are beginning their investigation of crystals.

0-87542-058-3
224 pp., illus., mass market $3.95

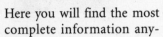

The Women's Book of Healing

Diane Stein

Diane Stein helps women (and men) reclaim their natural right to be healers with exercises to help you become a healer! Learn about the uses of color, vibration, crystals and gems for healing, the auric energy field, and the Chakras.

The book teaches alternative healing theory and techniques and combines them with crystal and gemstone healing, laying on of stones, psychic healing, laying on of hands, chakra work and aura work, and color therapy. It teaches beginning theory in the aura, chakras, colors, creative visualization, meditation, health theory and ethics with some quantum theory. Forty-six gemstones plus clear quartz crystals are discussed in detail, arranged by chakras and colors.

The Women's Book of Healing is designed to teach basic healing (Part I) and healing with crystals and gemstones (Part II). The remainder of the book discusses, in chakra-by-chakra format, specific gemstones for healing work, their properties and uses.

0-87542-759-6
352 pp., 6 x 9, illus., softcover $14.95